TEACHING
THE ELEMENTARY SCHOOL
CHORUS

TEACHING
THE ELEMENTARY SCHOOL
CHORUS

Linda Swears

Parker Publishing Company, Inc.
West Nyack, New York 10995

© 1985 by
PARKER PUBLISHING COMPANY, INC.
West Nyack, NY

Sixth Printing ..... September, 1989

Library of Congress Cataloging in Publication Data

Swears, Linda.
 Teaching the elementary school chorus.

 Includes index.

 1. Choral singing, Juvenile—Instruction and study.
2. School music—Instruction and study—United States.
I. Title.
MT930.S9 1985   372.8'73   84-16656

ISBN 0-13-892514-3

Printed in the United States of America

To my mother, father, and grandmother for the gift of music; to my uncle for the encouragement to write; and to my husband, Tom, for his love and support.

ABOUT THE AUTHOR

Linda Swears, B.M., M.A., is a music specialist at the Albert Einstein Academy in Wilmington, Delaware. She has been a music educator for fourteen years, during which time her children's choirs have performed on television and radio and at many professional conferences. Mrs. Swears has served as a state and division-level chairperson for the Music Educators National Conference and is a frequent clinician and workshop leader in the areas of the child voice and children's choirs. She is a published composer of choral music for children and the author of the children's book, *Discovering the Guitar*.

A WORD FROM THE AUTHOR

This book is written for anyone who teaches choral music. If you are an elementary choral teacher, you will find hundreds of practical suggestions for "what" and "how" to organize and teach your school chorus. If you are a junior high school, high school, or college teacher, you will gain new insights into the development of the child voice and the importance of establishing the foundation of choral singing in the elementary school.

IT ADDRESSES TEACHERS' CONCERNS

Until now, little has been written about teaching choral music at this level. Likewise, most college methods courses do not deal with the specific problems of working with young singers. This is ironic, since such a large number of vocal music teachers in schools in this country teach elementary school students and are responsible for organizing and directing some type of choral program. Over the years, it has become apparent to me that these teachers feel inadequately prepared for this task. They want to know where and how they can learn more about the child voice. They are anxious to learn of methods and materials that will "work" with young singers. In short, they want to know how they can more effectively teach their choral programs. *Teaching the Elementary School Chorus* is addressed to teachers with concerns such as these.

Throughout this book the term "choral teacher" will be used in place of "director" alone. This is because the successful director of any young choir must first be a knowledgeable and able teacher. The ability to relate to and communicate with youngsters is of primary importance in developing a good choral program.

IT IS DIVIDED INTO THREE SECTIONS

For easy reference, this book is divided into three sections: Building a Choral Music Program for Children, Achieving a Good

Choral Sound, and Planning for Successful Rehearsal and Performance.

Section One focuses on the problems of organizing and developing an elementary chorus. Discussion of the characteristics of the elementary-age child and the successful choral teacher is followed by guidelines for establishing goals and objectives for the choral program. Practical suggestions for long-range planning, gaining administrative and community support, scheduling, financing, and building student interest can all be found in Chapter 1. Suggestions for developing a Choral Teacher's Notebook are also included.

Chapter 2 begins with a discussion of the development of the child voice from birth to early adolescence. Many suggestions are offered to help develop the child voice to its fullest potential. Several practical approaches for evaluating vocal ability are given as well as many concrete suggestions for identifying and working with underdeveloped singers.

In Section Two you will find over 100 teaching strategies for achieving a good choral sound. Ideas for teaching the fundamentals of good posture, breathing, diction, tone quality, balance, blend, and intonation are found here. Also included are several effective ways to teach part singing. All in all, Chapters 3–6 will help insure the most expressive and enjoyable singing possible for your students.

As shown in Section Three, organizing a successful rehearsal begins with careful planning based on appropriate learning objectives. Chapter 7 will help you develop successful lesson plans as well as give you many rehearsal techniques appropriate for your young chorus. Special tips for working with large groups are also offered.

Preparing children for a choral concert or school program means detailed planning from start to finish. In Chapter 8 you will find a step-by-step guide to concert preparation beginning with complete guidelines for selecting the best music for your choir. Suggestions for program building are followed by ideas for concert themes and sample programs. Lists of music that have been particularly successful with children's choirs are also included in this chapter.

In Chapter 9, you will find information about developing conducting skills and suggestions for selecting and working with an accompanist. This chapter also includes helpful information for those who work with children in primary school, church, or community choirs. The section concludes with a compilation of resources related to teaching the elementary school chorus. Lists of publishers, recommended books, and suggestions for learning more about teaching children's choirs can be found here.

It is my intent that elementary choral teachers will use this book as a handy reference for any aspect of the elementary choral program. Beyond this, however, it is also my hope that, through good choral instruction, as many children as possible will grow into adults who love to sing and who have developed their singing skills to the fullest potential.

Linda Swears

ACKNOWLEDGMENTS

I thank Dr. Donald Regier, supervisor of Secondary Vocal Music in Baltimore County, Maryland, for his assistance and for the use of a variety of resources through his office; Mary Drawbaugh and Anna Leidich for proofreading the original text; Carole Miles for proofing the musical examples; Judy Miller and Sharon Davis for typing the manuscript; and the staff of the Talbott Library of Westminster Choir College for their excellent sleuthing.

CONTENTS

A Word from the Author vii

SECTION ONE
BUILDING A CHORAL MUSIC PROGRAM FOR CHILDREN

CHAPTER 1
Organizing the Elementary School Chorus 3

Before You Begin–3
Establishing Personal and Instructional Goals–7
The Choral Teacher's Notebook–8
Scheduling–9
Recruiting Administrative, Staff, and Parent Support–15
Determining Who Will Sing in the Chorus–17
Recruiting Chorus Members–19
Financing the Elementary School Chorus–21

CHAPTER 2
Understanding and Working with the Child Voice 25

The Development of the Child Voice–25
Evaluating Vocal Skills–34
The Underdeveloped Singer–37

SECTION TWO
DEVELOPING A FINE CHILDREN'S CHOIR

CHAPTER 3
Foundations of Good Choral Singing 51

   The Role of the Choral Teacher–51
   Teaching Children to Listen–59
   The Importance of Head Voice–62
   Developing Good Singing Posture–66
   Proper Breathing for Singing–70

CHAPTER 4
Understanding and Teaching Diction for Singing 75

   The Teacher's Reference to Diction–75
   How to Teach Diction for Singing–83

CHAPTER 5
Refining the Choral Sound 100

   Developing Good Tone Quality–100
   Balance and Blend for Children's Choirs–104
   Developing Good Intonation–108
   Teaching Children to Sing Expressively–112
   A Cappella Singing–115

CHAPTER 6
How to Teach Part Singing 118

   Teaching Ostinatos and Rounds–118
   Teaching Echo-Type Songs–126
   Teaching Songs with Countermelodies–127
   Teaching Partner Songs–129
   Teaching Two-, Three-, and Four-Part
   Vertical Harmony–130
   More Suggestions for Teaching Part Singing–138

SECTION THREE
PLANNING FOR SUCCESSFUL REHEARSAL AND PERFORMANCE

CHAPTER 7
Organizing the Successful Rehearsal **143**

Developing Rehearsal Objectives–143
Rehearsal Techniques–147
Classroom Management–152
Planning Special Rehearsals and Activities–156

CHAPTER 8
Concert Preparation **161**

Selecting Appropriate Music for the Elementary School
Chorus–161
Concert Themes and Program Building–169
Step-By-Step Pre-Concert Planning–174
Planning for Special Performances–179

CHAPTER 9
Other Responsibilities of the Choral Teacher **185**

Conducting the Elementary School Chorus–185
The Accompanist–191
Organizing Other Singing Experiences for Children–194
Developing Professional Resources–199

Index **205**

BUILDING A CHORAL MUSIC PROGRAM FOR CHILDREN

*Since singing is so good a thing,
I wish all men would learn to sing.*

William Byrd

Chapter 1
Organizing the Elementary School Chorus

BEFORE YOU BEGIN

Before you begin to organize or teach an elementary school chorus, three important questions should be asked:

1. Why teach choral singing in the elementary school?
2. Who are my students?
3. What skills and qualities do I need to be an effective elementary choral teacher?

Why teach choral singing in the elementary school? Is it because a principal or supervisor has determined there should be a school chorus to perform for special programs? Is it because there has always been a chorus and everyone expects it? Is it because of a need for joint planning time for classroom teachers, making the music class so large that a sing-a-long or chorus is the only feasible activity? Perhaps it is to provide an opportunity for working with more talented students.

Undoubtedly, most elementary school choruses exist for one or more of these reasons. The primary purpose for organizing a school chorus and teaching choral singing in the elementary school, however, should be to help children develop their fullest singing potential.

Learning to sing at one's best should be the right of every youngster. Unfortunately, the elementary general music class does not always provide the type of vocal emphasis needed to insure the development of accurate, expressive singers. With so much to be taught and so little time, singing often becomes a tool for teaching other musical skills and concepts.

3

While good singing habits should be taught at every opportunity from kindergarten throughout the elementary school years, there comes a time, usually between the ages of nine and twelve, when most children are ready to go beyond the singing games and activities of the general music class. They are physically, emotionally, and intellectually ready for more challenging singing experiences. Children who are not challenged at this critical stage often lose interest in singing as the difficult changes of adolescence begin.

The elementary school chorus provides an excellent opportunity for these upper elementary students to develop their singing potential. Within the large group, children can explore their vocal abilities without fear of personal failure or competition. As a part of a special group, they are usually highly motivated to do their best. As they learn the basics of singing posture, breath control, diction, phrasing, tone color, dynamics, and part singing they expand their singing skills and general musicianship as well.

Of course, there are other reasons for teaching choral singing in the elementary school. Together with the primary purpose stated above, these should become the broad goals of any elementary school choral program. They include:

1. Helping children develop a means of aesthetic expression and appreciation;

2. Helping children develop a varied repertoire of vocal literature including folk songs, art songs, sacred songs, songs of other cultures, and songs of the current genre;

3. Helping children understand the importance of corporate as well as personal experience and identity;

4. Helping children experience the joy and satisfaction of performing well for themselves and others; and

5. Helping children develop skills and attitudes that will encourage them to use their singing voices as lifelong musical instruments.

Notice that each of these goals begins with the phrase "helping children." To be truly effective, choral music in the elementary school must be child-centered. Singing for the sake of music or performance alone has little lasting value. But singing for the sake of children who grow into well-rounded adults, achieving their fullest human potential, is an end that deserves the choral teacher's utmost care and commitment.

Who are my students? No matter what age group you teach, it is important to view children in the context of their overall development. Understanding where a child has been and where he or she is going is essential in planning for optimum growth and development.

As you look at the continuum in Figure 1–1 be aware that children do not always fit neatly into these categories. In some schools the entire developmental scheme may be shifted ahead or behind because of ethnic background or environmental factors. In addition, it is important to remember that every child is unique. While the general physical and emotional characeristics given here are helpful, they are so only to the extent that they help us appreciate and value the individual child.

General Developmental Characteristics of Children
in Grades 1–8

Grades 1 and 2

Very active, love to run, jump, hop and skip; cannot sit for long periods of time; are easily fatigued.

Enjoy having rules to follow; like some regimentation.

Have vivid imaginations, enjoy pretending.

Look for approval from adults; need acceptance and encouragement from adults.

Time of rapid growth; tend to move whole body as a unit, but hands, arms, and feet are beginning to function with greater independence; front teeth will usually be missing sometime during this period.

Sense of tonality developing for many children; there is a wide diversity in vocal development.

Grades 3 and 4

Active but attention span increasing.

Conscious of right and wrong; developing ability to evaluate themselves and others, enjoy being part of a group.

Enjoy imaginative activities; enjoy folklore and have interest in patriotism; enjoy humor, adventure, and anything new.

Figure 1–1

Tendency to hero worship; strong need for adult models; need for encouragement and praise from adults and peers.

Physical growth slows somewhat; small muscle development allows for more detailed work.

Most children have developed a sense of tonality allowing for more accurate singing in an expanded range of about c^1 to e^2.

Grades 5 and 6

Variance in levels of maturity; girls generally more physically developed than boys.

Energetic and curious; able to concentrate on a given task for an extended time.

Can see humor in many situations; may tend to be giddy or silly at times.

Peer pressure becoming strong influence; want to be part of a group or gang; acceptance by others is very important.

Ability to evaluate the performance of themselves and others is increasing.

The child voice is usually at its peak of development, allowing for accurate, expressive singing.

Grades 7 and 8

Great variance in levels of physical and emotional maturity; girls generally more physically developed than boys; both may be awkward.

Energetic; love excitement and adventure.

Moods tend to fluctuate sharply; emotional behavior may appear very inconsistent.

Strong need for social acceptance and status within a group; tendency to hero worship.

Able to evaluate performance of self and others; tend to be very critical.

Wide diversity in vocal range and quality; many boys experiencing voice change.

Figure 1–1, continued

What skills and qualities do I need to be an effective elementary school choral teacher? Like any good teacher, you must understand the subject matter and be able to communicate it to students in some meaningful way. It is important to enjoy your work and feel a sense of pride about what you are doing. You should feel that your work is valuable and contributes something to society.

Regarding specific skills and knowledge, the elementary choral teacher should meet the following criteria:

1. Understands and interprets musical notation accurately and expressively,
2. Understands vocal production and technique,
3. Has specific knowledge of the qualities and limitations of the child voice,
4. Conducts with clarity and expressiveness, and
5. Possesses adequate organizational skills for planning and implementing the choral program.

Beyond this, you should have certain personal qualities that enable you to work effectively with children. Children will not automatically respond to good musicianship on the teacher's part. There must be an attitude of caring that permeates the student-teacher relationship.

Therefore, musical knowledge and skill are most effectively shared with children when the choral teacher:

1. Likes children and believes teaching them is an important task,
2. Possesses a healthy sense of humor,
3. Is confident of his or her musicianship and his or her person,
4. Exhibits warmth and acceptance toward students,
5. Recognizes the limitations and potential of students, and
6. Is as concerned with the process of learning as the product of learning.

ESTABLISHING PERSONAL AND INSTRUCTIONAL GOALS

Along with the broad goals stated earlier in this chapter, you will also need to determine personal and instructional goals that pertain to your particular situation. Personal goals will include anything you want to accomplish that is not directly related to instruction. These might include some of the following:

- Organizing a choral library,
- Recruiting parents to help with chorus activities,
- Improving your conducting skills,
- Organizing a special television performance.

Instructional goals should be child-centered and should be stated as direct outcomes of instruction. They should be statements of what you hope children will achieve as members of the chorus. Some important instructional goals might include:

- As chorus members, children will learn and demonstrate the fundamentals of good breath control for singing.
- As chorus members, children will gain enough confidence and skill to sing their parts independently and in small ensembles.
- As chorus members, children will learn and demonstrate the fundamentals of good diction for singing.

Whatever your goals may be, put them on paper and keep them handy as you begin to plan. Well-thought-out goals will be an important key to successful long-range and daily planning.

THE CHORAL TEACHER'S NOTEBOOK

As you begin to plan for your chorus, it is a good idea to organize a special notebook for only chorus matters. This can be any type of loose-leaf binder that will allow you to compile lists, schedules, music, and any odds and ends that pertain to the choral program. Include a clip-on pen or pencil, plenty of loose-leaf paper, graph paper, several dividers, and a calendar.

In the front of the notebook place a single sheet of paper listing your goals and objectives. Keep this in the front of the notebook so you can refer to it as you select music and plan daily lessons. Next, divide the notebook into sections labeled Lesson Plans, Music, Seating Chart, Role Chart, Calendar, Forms and Notices, Expenditures, Vocalises, and/or any other categories that may be helpful to you.

Obviously, the section labeled Lesson Plans will hold your lessons for chorus rehearsals. Good written lessons are as essential to the chorus rehearsal as they are in any classroom. Detailed suggestions for writing and implementing effective lessons will be given in Chapter 7.

Keeping your music in one place and in a specific order can often save time in rehearsal and when planning. You may want to use a hole puncher to actually fasten a copy of your music into the notebook, or you may want to keep music in a pocket of the notebook.

Be sure to include a seating chart and a list of chorus members in your notebook. Make the list on sheets of graph paper and use it as a check-off sheet when permission slips are returned or music is distributed or collected. You may want to keep attendance records here also.

A calendar should be an essential part of your notebook. Record here all special school activities, holidays, and choral events as soon as you are aware of them. By maintaining an up-to-date calendar, you can plan more efficiently and avoid conflicts when scheduling chorus activities.

Keep copies of all notices, permission slips, hand outs, and forms in another section. If questions should arise about these from your students or parents, you will have ready access to them.

In the section under Expenditures, keep track of all monies spent and received. Keep a ledger for yourself even though financial matters may be handled by the school office or music office. Keep copies of all bills, invoices, and orders here or in a special file.

It is also a good idea to keep a list of usable vocalises in your notebook. Because it is easy to forget these if they are not written down, jot ten or twelve good exercises on staff paper and refer to them as you plan. This list should be added to whenever you come across a new exercise you think appropriate for your group. As you plan, simply refer to this section to find vocal exercises that will help you accomplish your objectives.

Depending on your situation, you may want to add to or delete from these suggestions. Perhaps you will use a completely different system of organization that works well for you. Whatever system you devise, it is important to keep your notebook up to date. In this way, you can be sure information and materials you use frequently will be at your fingertips.

SCHEDULING

Once your notebook is in order, glance over your chorus calendar and begin to set some tentative dates. When will you meet with your principal to discuss plans and schedules for the coming year? When will you need to submit budget requests? When will you begin vocal assessments of your students? When will chorus begin? What are the dates of traditional school programs? What additional performances and activities will the chorus participate in? When will you need to order music to insure its arrival in plenty of time for study before a concert?

With these items tentatively penciled on your calendar, make an appointment to meet with your principal. Take along an extra copy of your goals and a tentative schedule to share with him or her. Once you have discussed your goals, together go over the proposed calendar date by date and be prepared to make some changes. A tentative schedule might look like the one in Figure 1–2.

Request that activities affecting students and other teachers be placed on an all-school calendar as soon as possible. Everyone involved will appreciate knowing these dates well in advance and you will have established some priority for chorus activities.

At this initial meeting, also be prepared to discuss rehearsal scheduling. It will be very helpful in gaining administrative support if you have well-defined goals and a rationale for the type of rehearsal schedule you feel necessary.

Scheduling Rehearsals

The full chorus rehearsal is the heart of any choral music program. As instructional time from which all other chorus activities emerge, it should be your top priority in scheduling. What you are able to accomplish in rehearsal is directly related to the amount and quality of time you have with your students.

Unfortunately, every school has its unique problems in scheduling and it is impossible to suggest a rehearsal schedule suitable in all situations. It is possible, however, to list some priorities for scheduling that should be shared with your administrator.

1. Because chorus provides an important learning experience, it should be scheduled during the school day.

2. Chorus should not be scheduled to take the place of recess, physical education, art, or instrumental music. These are all important experiences for the elementary school child, who should not have to give one up for the other.

3. Ideally, the elementary school chorus should meet twice a week for thirty-five to forty minutes. Two short rehearsals are suggested rather than one longer rehearsal because:

Tentative Chorus Schedule for the School Year

May	Discuss scheduling, financing, and rehearsal room assignment with principal.
June	Review new music for possible use.
August	Finalize rehearsal schedule and as many performance dates as possible. Order new music.
September	Prepare student calendars. Post chorus bulletin board. Initial voice assessments (Sept. 11–15). First rehearsal (Sept. 18).
October	Begin winter holiday music (Oct. 1). Happy Halloween rehearsal (Oct. 30).
November	Perform for Thanksgiving Assembly (Nov. 24).
December	Special holiday rehearsal (Dec. 15 in auditorium). Dress rehearsal (Dec. 16 in auditorium). Holiday Program (Dec. 17, 7:30 P.M.). Sing at Exton Mall (Dec. 20, 2:00 P.M.).* Caroling Party (Dec. 21, 6:30 P.M.).*
January	Begin work on mid-winter and spring music. Happy Birthday rehearsal (Jan. 30).
February	Chorus field trip to hear the Exton High School rehearsal of *The Music Man* (February 27).*
March	Music in Our Schools Week (March 15–20), parents and community invited to rehearsals; Mini Concert (March 20, 2:00 P.M.).
April	Perform for Music Educators Conference (April 20).
May	Spring Concert Rehearsal (May 14, in auditorium). Spring Concert Rehearsal (May 15, in auditorium). Spring concert (May 15, 7:30 P.M.). Area Choral Festival (May 31, Daley Junior High School).
June	Perform for Honors Assembly (June 7).

*Tentative dates, to be confirmed as soon as possible.

Figure 1–2

    a. Children retain more when they meet more frequently.

    b. The level of energy and concentration needed in the chorus rehearsal is difficult to maintain for a long period of time.

    c. With such a large number of students, discipline problems are less likely to occur in the shorter rehearsal.

    d. If a rehearsal is missed for some reason, an entire "week" of instruction is not lost.

    e. It is difficult to build student-to-student and student-to-teacher rapport in one class period a week. A good choral experience involves the development of a corporate identity that is almost impossible to achieve in a once-a-week rehearsal.

4. Chorus should be scheduled in an area adequate to comfortably handle the number of students enrolled and to provide an optimum learning environment.

Resolving Special Problems

Because of the numbers of students involved and the nature of most elementary school schedules, finding adequate rehearsal time and facilities may be difficult. Some special scheduling problems might be resolved by using one of the following suggestions:

1. If your school is very large, you may have to schedule chorus in two or three sections. This is not desirable, but it is feasible. In this type of situation be sure that all sections are able to rehearse together from time to time. If you have a very large number of students when sections are combined, ask for assistance from your administration or parent volunteers. Avoid teaching one section as altos and another as sopranos. While this might be done occasionally, children who sing only unison in rehearsal miss all the benefits of hearing and singing harmony.

2. Another alternative in large schools is to have a school chorus of students who want to sing, a smaller select chorus of more advanced students, and a training chorus.

3. In some schools, chorus is scheduled before or after school. If busing and other activities do not interfere, this may be your only alternative. Teachers who are required to teach beyond the regular school day should be compensated financially or with equal preparation time during the school day.

4. In some situations there may be absolutely no time in the school schedule for chorus. In this case you might try creating a special time for teaching "Vocal Technique and Choral Singing" in the general music class. Perhaps at this time the class seating arrangement is changed. Special chorus folders are distributed, and specific attention is given to singing. Children who choose to participate in performances might be issued membership cards for "Performing Choir," while children who choose not to perform still benefit from such emphasis on vocal production.

5. Don't be afraid to ask for help in scheduling. Others are often able to see possibilities you may not have considered. Obtain schedules from other elementary schools to see how chorus fits into their schedules. Ask a music supervisor to share good rehearsal schedules he or she has observed in other schools. Does your supervisor see scheduling possibilities you are not aware of? Also, ask for input from classroom teachers whose students will be involved in chorus. They may have helpful suggestions you have not considered.

Scheduling Sectionals and Special Groups

Unless you have a very flexible schedule, sectionals and additional rehearsal times for special groups may be difficult to arrange. Efficient all-chorus rehearsals can minimize the need for sectionals, but occasionally they are helpful. Several possibilities for securing this additional time include:

1. Arrange a "flex" period in your teaching schedule. This is a time slot (15–30 minutes) each day when you can work with small groups of students, sectionals, or program preparation.

2. Schedule sectional rehearsals during the regular chorus rehearsal. Ask a parent or volunteer to conduct the sectional. If you do not have a musically competent person willing to help, make rehearsal tapes and ask volunteers to supervise while students rehearse with the tape.

3. Arrange mini-sectionals before school, after school, or during transition time during the school day.

Scheduling Voice Assessments

It is best to schedule individual or small group assessment times early in the school year before chorus begins. If you are the general music teacher as well as the choral teacher, it is a good idea to listen to all children eligible for chorus membership. For instance, if chorus is open to all interested 5th- and 6th-level students, try to listen to all of these students, not just those interested in chorus. You are likely to discover many lovely voices and to develop a more personal rapport with all your students.

Ask students to sign up for voice assessments on a schedule you have posted. Times can usually be arranged before school, at lunch or recess, and after school. Ideally, time scheduled for chorus can be used before rehearsals actually begin. Assessments need only take about ten minutes.

Scheduling Performances

The performance schedule of the elementary school chorus should be planned with several factors in mind. First, concerts should be spaced to allow adequate preparation of new music. Too little time between concerts can be frustrating if new music must be learned. At the same time, concerts appropriately spaced can provide motivation for learning.

Another idea is to plan performances in clusters based on your repertoire. For instance, in December when your holiday repertoire is ready, try to perform at least two or three times. After the winter holidays, begin to concentrate on a repertoire of varied numbers that can be used for mid-winter and spring performances. One or two mid-winter performances should be planned to help maintain group morale and motivate learning. Likewise, at least one late spring concert using some new material should be planned to encourage optimum growth throughout the entire school year.

Try to schedule a variety of musical performances with some being more demanding than others. In December this might include the full school concert followed by an informal sing at a local mall. In the spring, this might include a school concert, a trip to a choral festival, and a short performance for a local club, hospital, or nursing home.

Finally, avoid conflicts in scheduling by referring to your school calendar, a community calendar, and the concert schedule of local junior and senior high schools. Because families may have children in different schools and involved in various musical activities, it is particularly important that you work with directors in other local schools to see that concert schedules do not conflict.

RECRUITING ADMINISTRATIVE, STAFF, AND PARENT SUPPORT

The support of administrators, staff, and parents will enhance your ability to provide a good educational program for your students. Their efforts can help insure good scheduling, adequate rehearsal facilities, money for music and choral activities, and good student morale.

No matter if your situation is one where choral music is highly valued or where choral music is considered a "frill," your own professional attitude will be the single most important factor in gaining or maintaining this needed support. A principal who has little appreciation for choral music may learn to value it through his or her appreciation of a capable and dedicated teacher. Parents who have never thought much about their children's singing skills may be delighted to discover what a difference your teaching has made in their children's attitudes and skill development.

In general, to gain the support of others, it is important to:

1. Be professional in your work. Let others know you value what you do and what they do.
2. Be organized and efficient. Time is the stuff of life and no one appreciates it being wasted. This includes students.
3. Be flexible. Stand up for your rights and make your position known, but be aware that things cannot always be your way.
4. Be a creative problem solver. When a problem arises, don't be the first to throw up your hands and quit. Train yourself to find at least two solutions to every "unsolvable" problem.

More specifically to gain the support of your school administrator, it is helpful to:

1. Inform him or her of your goals and objectives.
2. Share ways the school chorus can enhance the overall school program.
3. Invite your principal or other administrators to concerts outside of school. Introduce them and ask them to say a few words on behalf of the school and chorus.
4. Invite administrators to rehearsals as well as concerts. Let them know you value rehearsal as much as performance.

5. Keep administrators informed of how students are progressing in chorus, particularly students with special learning or emotional problems. Often chorus will be a positive experience for these students and can provide an impetus for success in other areas.

6. Plan carefully, helping to avoid last minute unscheduled rehearsals or performances.

The support of your teaching colleagues is especially helpful in building personal and student morale. To gain their support:

1. Work as a staff member. If you are considered a "specialist," don't be so special that you forget you are part of a team working to insure the best overall education for your students.

2. Support the programs and projects of other teachers. Goodwill is usually reciprocal.

3. Let others know you appreciate them. When other staff members lend a helping hand, be sure they receive deserved recognition and a warm thank you.

4. Avoid unexpected activities that disrupt the school day. Let teachers know well in advance when the chorus will perform or rehearse.

Good parental support can be a tremendous help to the elementary choral teacher. Administrators are strongly influenced by parent opinion and elementary age children usually share their values. In short, good parental support can be a major factor in establishing a successful choral program. To gain parent support:

1. Identify and meet with parent leaders to discuss goals and plans for the school chorus.

2. Organize a group of "chorus parents" to help with rehearsals, performances, special activities, and field trips. Meet with and call these parents periodically.

3. Invite parents to rehearsals as well as concerts.

4. Present teaching demonstrations as well as performances at parent-teacher meetings.

Above all, to recruit the support of others, be sure your intentions are child-centered. Administrators, staff, and parents are most likely to support your program if they sense it is child-centered and designed to help children reach their fullest potential.

DETERMINING WHO WILL SING IN THE CHORUS

Before you actually begin recruiting chorus members, it is important to determine who will be eligible to sing. Obviously, in most situations, every child in the school will not be able to participate in one chorus. Numbers of students, scheduling, and restricted rehearsal facilities usually make it necessary for the choral teacher to limit chorus enrollment in some way.

First, it is important to consider who will benefit most from choral instruction. As we have seen, because of physical, emotional, and intellectual development, this will most likely be upper elementary students. This is not to say that younger children cannot benefit from singing in a chorus, but rather that upper elementary children are usually at a more appropriate readiness level. Limiting chorus to the upper grades also sets it apart as something special that children can look forward to. Preparing for chorus in the lower grades can be a good motivating factor for younger children as they develop vocal skills. This also helps set up an objective method for determining who may participate without simply selecting the "best" singers.

The elementary chorus should be as inclusive as possible, never excluding a child because he or she doesn't sing well. All children need as much singing experience as possible and can benefit greatly from the attention placed on vocal skills in the school chorus. Telling a child he or she may not participate in chorus because he or she does not sing well is a sure way to stifle further vocal development.

Some people argue that "out-of-tune" singers ruin the sound of the chorus and deprive more talented students from doing their best. While these arguments may have some merit with older, select performing groups, remember that the primary purpose of the elementary school chorus is to help children "develop their fullest singing potential." For some children, this may mean simply learning to sing on pitch. Often times, children who are late in developing vocal skills will make tremendous progress in chorus. At the same time, more advanced students should be encouraged to be tolerant of those who are not as skilled. The overall attitude in chorus should be one that encourages all children to do their best while accepting and helping one another. Many specific suggestions for working with these under-developed singers can be found in Chapter 2.

Providing for More Advanced Students

If you have a fair number of rather advanced singers, is it possible to organize a special or extracurricular group for them? From most choruses of sixty to seventy members, this will involve fifteen or twenty students who are capable of more challenging work. This would be a select group with membership by audition and/or invitation.

By organizing this group as an outgrowth of the school chorus, you are able to include as many students as possible in the overall choral program, while still providing special learning opportunities for advanced students. The basic selection for this group should occur early in the school year with the possible addition of several new members throughout the year. As you identify children who seem capable of more advanced work, be flexible enough to accept them into the group. This approach, rather than to discourage students who are not initially selected, often motivates students to do their best in hopes of becoming a part of the special group.

The select ensemble might perform two or three more difficult numbers during a full chorus concert. They might represent the school at functions where a large performing group is not feasible. In this situation their repertoire can be a combination of music learned in chorus and in the ensemble rehearsal.

As with the chorus, the purpose of the smaller select group should be to help children develop their singing potential. Therefore, these students should be challenged not only by the literature they perform, but also by your expectations for their individual vocal development.

How Large Should the Chorus Be?

A good size for an elementary chorus is usually between forty-five and eighty members. With more than eighty, discipline as well as adequate materials and rehearsal area usually becomes a problem. The ideal size of about fifty to sixty students usually results in a good choral sound, optimum learning, and good teacher and student morale.

RECRUITING CHORUS MEMBERS

Elementary-age children like to participate in special groups and activities. While younger children will often join a particular group "just for the fun of it," older students (grades 4, 5, and 6) want to be sure the group is worthwhile. They want to know what, when, and why before they commit themselves. Boys, especially, must be assured belonging is not considered "sissy."

Tradition and reputation are two very valuable aids in recruiting youngsters for chorus. If there has been a strong choral program in the school for several years, many students will want to participate because it is "the thing to do." If older brothers and sisters have participated in and valued the choral experience, it is most likely younger brothers and sisters will be eager to participate.

Bulletin Boards

At the beginning of the year, be sure the music room or one of the hall bulletin boards is devoted to information about chorus. Include the date of the first rehearsal and some of the concerts and special activities that are planned. The board should be colorful and attractive. Including several pieces of music you plan to perform will also help to generate interest.

Choristers Guild has several colorful recruiting posters designed especially for elementary-age choirs. Themes of some of the posters include, "Free Tune-Ups," "Don't Be a Lone Wolf....Join the Choir and Sing with the Pack," and "Wanted." These commercially prepared posters are delightful and can be ordered from Choristers Guild whose address you will find in Chapter 9.

Voice Assessments

Voice assessments can provide an opportunity for recruitment at a more personal level. Building a child's confidence in these small groups or private sessions is often all that is needed to encourage participation in chorus.

As you would expect, children who have pleasant voices and enjoy singing usually need little encouragement to join chorus. Children who demonstrate little vocal ability and lack confidence about singing, however, will need all the encouragement you can give. Let these children know you want to help them and that you believe, through chorus and special work, they can become better singers. Let these children know chorus will be a "safe" place for them. They will not be singled out or ridiculed if they do not sing on pitch all the time.

The Pre-Chorus Rehearsal

Another way to build student interest is to hold a "pre-chorus" rehearsal. Anyone interested in joining chorus is invited to attend. Here you discuss the various concerts and activities planned, expectations for chorus participation, and a preview of some of the music to be learned. One very effective technique is to show a slide presentation of what the previous year's chorus did and accomplished.

This presentation should be prepared throughout each year of chorus. Ask a student photographer or a chorus parent to take photos at the first rehearsal and at all concerts and special activities through the year. Likewise, assign someone to tape segments of the first rehearsal, special activities, and concerts. As the end of the year approaches, assign a willing committee to edit and prepare the presentation. Depending on the abilities of your students, this is a "fun" project for those who are media-inclined. The presentation should be kept from year to year and the producers should, of course, receive credit. The presentation can be as simple or elaborate as students wish. It is a good idea, however, to limit the presentation to no more than twenty minutes. If you do not have students who are capable, ask a parent, colleague, or administrator to organize this for you.

Be sure during the pre-chorus session that you are very specific about expectations for chorus. Elementary-age children want and need to know the standards of behavior and performance you expect. They will respond to firm but fair management and prefer to be in groups where expectations are high and praise is plentiful. Be sure children realize chorus is not recess or play time. It is a time for hard work, but work that is special and very rewarding.

Recruiting Boys

Unfortunately, in some schools and communities, singing in a chorus is considered "sissy" by the boys. This attitude is difficult to overcome and is best avoided by building a strong singing program from kindergarten through grade six within the general music class. If children have learned to enjoy singing in the primary grades and are challenged appropriately to develop their singing skills throughout elementary school, this attitude rarely develops.

However, if this is a problem in your school, here are some tips for handling it.

1. Set high expectations for chorus participation.
2. Compare the skills and attitudes needed for a chorus to those needed in developing a good athletic team.
3. Invite a group of high school or college age male singers to demonstrate or perform at your school. This is especially helpful when they have been former members of your chorus.
4. Encourage fathers to participate as chorus parents. Try to identify fathers who enjoy singing and occasionally invite them to rehearsals to assist you.
5. Is there a male member of the faculty who is respected by the students and enjoys singing? Invite him to sing a solo with the chorus or, at least, to help out occasionally.
6. Strive to interest several boys who are leaders in the school. Often if one or two leaders decide to join chorus, other boys will follow their lead.
7. Show an open respect for all types of music from rock to the classics. Boys are especially turned-off by music teachers who know nothing about current popular music.
8. Openly let it be known you are seeking several outstanding students to serve as section leaders in chorus. Let it be known you need both boys and girls to fill these positions.
9. Discuss the special qualities of the boy voice and how it will change with maturation. Stimulating interest in singing and the voice are forerunners to interest in chorus participation.

FINANCING THE ELEMENTARY SCHOOL CHORUS

Making a Budget Proposal

Begin financial planning by asking, "How much money is needed to provide the best program of instruction?" Initially, do not be concerned with where this money will come from. Simply try to determine actual costs based on materials needed to meet your instructional objectives. A tentative budget might look like Figure 1–3.

The Greenwood School Chorus Budget Proposal for the School Year	
1. Sixty chorus music folders (60 × $.35 per folder)	$21.00
2. Three S.A. selections for the holiday program (3 × 60 copies × $.75 per copy)	$135.00
3. Bus money to perform at the Greenwood Mall (2 buses at $40.00 each)	$80.00
4. Two S.A. selections for the mid-winter concert (2 × 60 copies × $.75 per copy)	$90.00
5. Music library fees for three selections for the spring concert (3 × 60 copies × $.10 per copy)	$18.00
6. Bus money for the area Choral Festival (2 buses at $40.00 each)	$80.00
7. End-of-the-year award certificates (60 awards × $.30 each)	$18.00
8. Miscellaneous teaching materials: (1 vowel chart) (4 posters at $2.50 each) (5 music storage boxes at $2.00 each)	$10.00 $10.00 $10.00
Total Budget	$472.00

Figure 1–3

At first, this total figure may seem high to teachers who have never estimated a choral budget. However, through careful and creative planning it may be quite possible for you to finance a similar proposal.

Sources of Financial Support

To obtain financial support begin by asking your administrator and/or music supervisor what monies are allocated for chorus in the school and/or music budgets. Beyond this, are there monies traditionally available to chorus but not necessarily a part of a formal budget? This might include funds from school or PTA fund raisers that are annually distributed to various school programs. Combined, these sources will probably provide the most money for your budget. It is likely, however, that they will not be adequate to meet all of your needs, so you may want to explore alternative ways of meeting your proposed budget.

At this point it is very important that you be familiar with your school and board of education fiscal policies. Never undertake any money raising activities without the approval of the appropriate administrator. Money is a very delicate matter and you may do your program a great deal of harm by failing to follow accepted procedures.

Once you have assessed your needs and reviewed accepted fiscal policy in your county or district, you may want to discuss some of the following suggestions with your principal.

Chorus Music Folders. Most students are able to afford a chorus folder for their music. Is it possible to order these through a school store, asking each student to pay $.30 or $.35 for the folder? Is there a music store in your area or state that might furnish folders free? Many music stores that stock choral music will do this to encourage you to order music from them. Investigate the possibility.

Financing Trips. Bus monies are another area that can sometimes be covered by students. Since most field trips are paid for by students, it is not surprising that some chorus trips might be financed this way. Does your school have a field trip fund? Does your county or area music office provide funds for performance trips? Check these possibilities before you decide field trips and outside-of-school performances are too expensive for your group.

Establishing Choral Libraries. The cost of good instructional music is usually the most expensive item in the choral budget. If your school has no choral library, this portion of your budget will be high until you have had an established library for three or four years. Once you have a basic library of twenty or thirty pieces, this amount can be reduced.

Establishing a system- or county-wide elementary choral library can be another tremendous money saver for choral teachers. With this system, choral music for area schools is purchased and kept in one central location. Schools may borrow the music at no cost or for a small service fee ($.10 per copy for three months). Monies received in this way can be used to buy new music for the library. Once a system like this is well establihsed, it can save you hundreds of dollars a year.

Obtaining General Funds. One effective way of obtaining general funds is the recruitment of community sponsors. Through this approach, local business and professional people make donations to the chorus as patrons. The names of these persons or businesses are included in concert programs along with a thank you for their support.

Using some of the suggestions presented here, Figure 1–4 shows how the budget proposed earlier might be met.

ITEM	*FUNDED BY:*
1. Chorus folders $21.00	Supplied at no charge by Lane Music Store
2. Choral music $243.00	School budget $50.00, music office $75.00, PTA $50.00, chorus patrons $68.00
3. Bus monies $160.00	School field trip fund $80.00, chorus patrons $80.00
4. Award certificates $18.00	PTA $18.00
5. Miscellaneous teaching materials $30.00	School budget $15.00 PTA $30.00
TOTAL NEEDED $472.00 Free chorus folders − 21.00 $451.00	TOTAL RECEIVED $466.00

Figure 1–4

Chapter 2
Understanding and Working with the Child Voice

THE DEVELOPMENT OF THE CHILD VOICE

The Preschool Years

Children learn to sing in the same manner they learn to speak—primarily through imitation. From birth, auditory stimulation becomes a vital ingredient in this process. As a child responds to sounds in the environment and seeks to express him- or herself vocally, the foundations of singing are laid.

Marvin Greenberg's research into the development of the child voice points out five important developmental stages young children experience as they learn to sing. These include (1) first vocalizations, (2) vocal experimentation and sound imitation, (3) the approximation of singing, (4) singing accuracy within a limited range, and (5) singing accuracy within an expanded range.[1] In optimum situations, Greenberg suggests the following:

Stage I
First Vocalizations
(Ages Birth to 3 Months)

From birth, the normal healthy child develops a repertoire of vocalizations that help him or her interact with the environment. The child's earliest cries, coos, and sighs form a basis for the development of all singing and spoken language.

---

[1]Marvin Greenberg, *Your Children Need Music.* Englewood Cliffs, NJ: Prentice-Hall, 1979, p. 56.

Stage II

Vocal Experimentation and Sound Imitation
(Ages 3 Months to 18 Months)

During this stage the child enjoys experimenting with his or her own vocalizations. Gurgles, squeals, and babbling are among the child's favorite utterances. Between six and nine months musical babbling may begin, especially when an adult or older child sings to the infant.

These musical babbles have definite pitch but usually lack a definite rhythm. Tones are frequently repeated, move in small intervals, or slide downward. Pitches appear to center around middle c^1 but can encompass as many as eight scale tones.

Stage III

The Approximation of Singing
(Ages 18 Months to 3 Years)

In this stage babbling takes on a new dimension as speech development progresses rapidly. "Babbling songs" emerge with more definite rhythm and wider pitch intervals.

At about age two or later the child can begin to learn songs he or she hears. Most often the child will first imitate words, then rhythmic patterns, and finally, pitches. With singing models and some adult guidance, most children can imitate simple songs by age three.

Stage IV

Singing Accuracy—Limited Range
(Ages 3 Years to 4 Years)

At about age three, children who have had many experiences approximating pitches of songs will begin to sing accurately in a range from about d^1 to g^1 above middle c^1. This is also a time of spontaneous singing and making up of original songs.

Stage V

Singing Accuracy—Expanded Range
(Ages 4 years and Up)

With many singing experiences and guidance, some children will be able to sing accurately in the range of middle c^1 to c^2 by the age of four or five.

While some children will experience these stages at about the ages Greenberg suggests, a few will complete them earlier, with most completing them sometime during elementary school. This is due to a variety of factors including (1) environment and exposure to singing models, (2) repeated opportunities for vocal experimentation and imitation, (3) physical and emotional maturation, (4) innate musical capacity, and (5) encouragement and guidance from adults who value singing.

Of primary importance in this developmental scheme is the approximation of singing stage usually occurring between the ages of about eighteen months and three years. At this time a repertoire of tonal patterns is being developed and tonal memory is being shaped. Unfortunately, the heavy emphasis on language development at this time may result in inattention to the development of the child's singing voice. For whatever reason, if singing is neglected at this stage, the result may be children and even adults who fail to achieve singing accuracy without remedial help.

Fortunately, vocal development is not strictly bound by time. Experience is the more important ingredient and as seen in the next section, a good program of vocal instruction in the elementary school can do a great deal to insure optimum vocal development for every child.

The Elementary School Years

While children may enter elementary school at various stages of vocal development, there are certain characteristics that can be observed in most children at a given grade level. Planning for continued vocal development in the elementary grades should take these characteristics into consideration while allowing for exceptional children at either end of the spectrum.

Characteristics of Kindergarten Singers

Children reach kindergarten and first grade with a wide variety of singing skills. Most will not sing "in tune" and as many as 50 percent may not demonstrate a difference when speaking or singing. Voice quality is usually light and airy, but there are exceptions, including children who yell when they attempt to sing. During vocal play children will exhibit a wide vocal range, perhaps as much as 2½ octaves. For most group singing experiences, however, the range of d¹ to a¹ is preferred. A sense of tonality is usually developing and children will often sing a song "around the tonic," while many pitches remain inaccurate. The concepts of high and low are not understood by most children and movement with singing occurs quite naturally. Children enjoy make-believe and song stories. Chants are an important part of the vocal repertoire.

The kindergarten teacher should not be surprised to find a wide diversity of singers in any given class. It is not uncommon to have children who (1) "sing" as they speak, (2) sing below pitch, (3) sing above pitch, (4) sing very loudly, (5) sing within a very limited range, and (6) children who are afraid to sing. With physical maturation, good instruction, and plenty of opportunities to sing, all of these children can become adequate singers.

Nurturing Vocal Development in Kindergarten. To help nurture appropriate vocal development in kindergarten, the teacher should:

1. Help children hear, feel, and demonstrate the difference between singing and speaking.
2. Allow many opportunities for independent improvisation, encouraging children to explore the variety of sounds they can make with their voices.
3. Plan singing activities that include and encourage movement.
4. Provide many opportunities for echoing and chanting, emphasizing short patterns using sol, mi, la, and do.
5. Pitch most songs and chants between d^1 and a^1 to help develop pitch accuracy in this limited range.
6. Encourage all children to sing alone as well as with others through singing games and dramatizations.
7. Encourage children to "match" their voices with others in group singing.
8. Through listening, movement, and graphics help children identify and sing simple ascending and descending melodies.
9. Provide a repertoire of songs and chants that children will enjoy singing in and out of school.
10. Provide a secure and encouraging atmosphere for singing.

Characteristics of First and Second Grade Singers

In first and second grade, some children will still need emphasis on the difference between singing and speaking. Most children will be good directional singers with many pitch-accurate singers emerging by the end of the second grade. The vocal range expands upward during these years allowing comfortable singing for most youngsters between c^1 and d^2.

Children still enjoy moving to music and especially enjoy song stories and plays. Language development at this stage enhances singing. Songs are learned more quickly and rhythmic accuracy improves significantly. Children are able to remember longer rhythmic and tonal patterns. By the end of second grade, tonality is becoming well established.

Children begin to develop a "feeling" for their singing voice at this stage. They become increasingly aware of singing "in tune" with others and are able to sing unison melodies quite well. At the end of the second grade some children will be capable of good independent singing.

Nurturing Vocal Development in Grades 1 and 2. Many of the suggestions offered for vocal development in kindergarten should continue through grades one and two. Readiness for certain activities is not automatic as children progress from grade to grade. Teachers must be sensitive to the needs of their students and determine what should be taught based on these needs.

To help nurture appropriate vocal development in grades one and two, the teacher should:

1. If needed, continue activities to help differentiate between singing and speaking.

2. Continue to use songs, games, and activities that include movement.

3. Provide many opportunities for chanting and echoing, frequently using students as leaders.

4. Pitch most singing between c^1 and d^2.

5. Encourage all students to sing alone as well as in groups through singing games and dramatizations.

6. Help children discover the expressive qualities of their voices through the use of varied dynamics, tone color, tempo, and phrasing.

7. Through listening, movement, and graphics help children identify and sing (a) ascending and descending melodies, (b) high and low sounds, (c) melodies that move by step or leap.

8. Begin to nurture the rudiments of singing in harmony by use of simple ostinatos.

9. Provide a repertoire of songs and chants that children will enjoy singing in school, at home, and with friends.

10. Increase auditory memory and tonal vocabulary by frequent repetition of more complex melodic patterns such as:

(a) s m | s s   l | s   m, (b) s   l sm d | d d dm s,

and (c) mm   s   mm d | mm l l   s.

Characteristics of Third and Fourth Grade Singers

With good vocal instruction and many opportunities for singing, most youngsters should sing on pitch most of the time by the end of third grade. Children are increasingly aware of pitch accuracy for themselves and others. A sense of tonality is established and the rudiments of singing in harmony usually begin. The vocal range is expanded upward from c^1 to about e^2 or f^2. Voice quality, especially in the upper tones, is developing clarity and purity. Tonal and rhythmic memory continues to increase, allowing more difficult music to be sung. Many children become independent singers during this time.

Nurturing Vocal Development in Grades 3 and 4. To nurture appropriate vocal development in grades three and four, the teacher should:

1. Plan activities to help children hear and feel the difference between chest and head voice.

2. Introduce children to the importance of good singing posture.

3. Introduce some rudiments of diction for singing, such as pronouncing words distinctly and stressing a more open mouth position when singing.

4. Help children to expand the singing range to include c^1 to e^2 or f^2.

5. Provide many experiences that will build confidence in independent and solo singing and encourage an accepting attitude toward all students and their singing ability.

6. Expand children's abilities to sing expressively by continued work with dynamics, tone color, tempo, and phrasing.

7. Emphasize the importance of beautiful unison singing. Encourage children to listen to themselves and others in group singing and to strive for a unified sound.

8. Nurture singing harmony through the use of ostinatos, descants, rounds, and simple two-part songs.

9. Provide a repertoire of songs that children will enjoy singing in school, at home, and with friends.

10. Increase auditory memory and the tonal vocabulary by introducing more complex rhythmic and tonal patterns. Listening to, singing and writing these patterns will help to reinforce them for students. It is important that these patterns be learned in sequence and that they build on previous patterns children already know.

11. Provide special singing opportunities for children, especially in grade four. Beginning or training choirs may be initiated effectively at this time.

12. Provide remedial small group or individual instruction for children who do not sing on pitch.

Characteristics of Fifth and Sixth Grade Singers

During fifth and sixth grade most children reach a peak of vocal development. This occurs just prior to adolescence and often results in a beautiful singing tone unique to the child voice.

Vocal timbre in head voice is usually clear and more resonant than in grades three and four. At the same time, rich chest tones may be developing. While individual vocal ranges will vary, many children sing accurately in a range from $b\flat$ to f^2.

Physical, intellectual, and emotional maturation work together at this age to foster more expressive singing. Greater breath control allows for more extended phrases and dynamic contrast. The ability to understand and perform the fundamentals of good diction improves tone quality and more accurate intonation. High physical and emotional energy enables students to perform more challenging music.

Many children are independent singers at this stage. Beautiful solo and unison singing is quite possible. At the same time, a harmonic sense is quickly developing and singing in harmony becomes an important developmental task.

Fifth and sixth graders are very sensitive about the quality of their singing. They are able to make judgments about their singing and the singing of others. They want to sing well and need challenge to develop their fullest singing potential.

Nurturing Vocal Development in Grades 5 and 6. For most children, grades five and six will be a time of optimum learning and performance with the child voice. Children who build confidence in their ability to sing at this stage are likely to have fewer vocal problems during adolescence and are likely to continue to use their singing voices as they mature.

To nurture appropriate vocal development in grades five and six, the teacher should:

1. Emphasize the importance of developing the head voice for good solo and group singing.

2. Provide activities that will help children understand and use proper posture and breathing for singing.

3. Introduce the fundamentals of good diction for singing. (See Chapter 4.)

4. Help children to expand the vocal range to include b♭ upward to f². (Some boys in the first stage of voice change may have difficulty with the upper part of this range. Do not force them to sing these pitches if it creates vocal strain.)

5. Help to expand children's abilities to sing expressively by continued work with dynamics, tone color, tempo, and phrasing.

6. Continue to emphasize the importance of beautiful unison singing. Clarify the role of the singer as a soloist and an ensemble member.

7. Expand children's abilities to sing harmony through more complex descants, ostinatos, rounds, and two- and three-part songs. Choose materials carefully for maximum learning. (See Chapter 8.)

8. Provide a repertoire of songs that children will enjoy singing in school, at home, and with friends. Select challenging but accessible music that will engage the whole child.

9. Increase auditory memory and tonal vocabulary through a continuation of listening, singing, and writing activities. It is important that these patterns be learned in sequence and that they build on previous patterns children already know.

10. Provide singing experiences that will challenge children. This is the most ideal age for initiating the school chorus and other vocal ensembles.

11. Continue to provide small group or individual instruction for students who do not sing on pitch.

12. Discuss voice change with all students. Help them to under-
    stand these changes are natural and that developing good
    vocal habits will make the change easier. Work in small groups
    with boys who are experiencing the first stages of change.

The Changing Voice

With the onset of adolescence, the child voice begins to change.
While this is true for girls as well as boys, the change is much more
marked for boys and may sometimes begin to occur as early as fifth and
sixth grade. This is especially true for older boys who have repeated a
grade. While the vast majority of changing voices emerge in grades 7, 8
and 9, the elementary teacher should be prepared to work with boys
whose voices begin to change and to help prepare them for the
changes that will occur as they mature.

While there is no predictable pattern of change for all boys, some
early signs the teacher may detect include: (1) a new husky or raspy
quality in the speaking voice, (2) a more brilliant quality in the color of
the singing voice, (3) an extension of the lower range of the voice, and
(4) loss of the top notes of the head voice. If and when you begin to
observe one or more of these changes in a boy's voice, arrange a time to
listen to him individually. If there are several boys whose voices are
changing, organize a special group to meet every two or three weeks to
evaluate what changes are taking place, to offer encouragement, and to
help boys learn how to use their emerging new voices. It is important to
keep tabs on these voices so you do not expect them to perform vocal
tasks they are incapable of. While it is important for boys to sing
throughout voice change, they should never be encouraged to strain or
force the voice. For this reason, it is often helpful to tell boys to sing
what they can sing comfortably and to omit notes that are uncomfortable for them. Encourage boys whose voices are changing to let you
know whenever they experience difficulty in singing.

While girls' voices undergo change also, it is much more subtle and
is perceived as part of a more gradual maturation. If you imagine the
difference in the vocal quality of a fifth grade girl and a female high
school senior, you will realize a significant change does occur between
elementary and high school. When compared to the boy's vocal change,
however, it is far less dramatic. Therefore, girls rarely need the special
attention boys do at this awkward time.

For teachers who do encounter changing voices in their elementary students, the following books and articles are recommended:

Teaching Junior High School Music by Irvin Cooper and Karl O. Kuersteiner. Boston: Allyn and Bacon, 1965.

Music Teaching in the Junior High and Middle School by Frederick Swanson. Englewood Cliffs, NJ: Prentice-Hall, 1973.

"The Development of a Contemporary, Eclectic Theory for the Training and Cultivation of the Junior High School Male Changing Voice," by J. Cooksey, an article from the *Choral Journal,* Oct., Nov., Dec. 1977, and Jan. 1978.

"The Changing Voice" by Mayer and Sacher from the *American Choral Review,* Vol. VI, Nos. 2 and 3.

EVALUATING VOCAL SKILLS

Good vocal evaluation should serve two purposes. First, it should help you become aware of your students' abilities and help you to plan for their continued vocal development. Second, it should help individual children become aware of their own unique voices.

During the evaluation, both teacher and student must be attentive. Just going through the motions will be of little benefit to either of you. For this reason, a one-to-one evaluation is usually best. In this situation, the teacher can devote specific attention to one student while the student need not worry about what peers are thinking of his or her performance. However, there are some children who feel more secure in a small group or with a friend during evaluation and this should be allowed if it is truly helpful to the student.

Very few people enjoy evaluation by others and children are no exception. Their egos are often fragile and the slightest negative comment may be perceived as total failure. Therefore, choose your words carefully. Be positive and encouraging. Your words will have a powerful effect on shaping the child's opinion of his or her voice.

Good vocal evaluation should be a learning experience for the teacher and student. Work together to discover the student's present skills, any problems, and his or her potential. Help the child to take pride in the skills he or she has and challenge the child to take some specific responsibility for further vocal development. For instance, if a child has poor singing posture that prevents good performance, challenge the child to improve his or her posture. Give the child specific instructions about singing posture and let him or her know you will be looking and listening for a change.

In general, the evaluation session should be viewed by students as a chance to determine what is needed to help them achieve their singing potential, not as a test one passes or fails. To do this successfully the child must know (1) you value him or her regardless of his or her present singing ability, (2) singing is something that can be learned, and (3) you will help the child in every way you can to become the best singer possible.

Preparing Students for Vocal Evaluation

No matter how you decide to structure your evaluation sessions, it is important that students understand what they will be expected to do and why. Begin by referring to the evaluation as an "interview." Help children understand that just as a regular interview can help you learn more about something or someone, a vocal interview can help you learn more about the student and his or her voice. Rehearse parts of the vocal interview in general music class or early chorus rehearsals. Let children know what you will be listening for. Let them see the "Vocal Interview" form (see Figure 2–1) you will be using and ask them to complete as much of it as possible before their interview.

To use the "Vocal Interview" form, have children complete the information at the top of the form and answer questions one and two. Complete the remaining portions in the interview as follows:

Range: To determine range, have children sing the pattern sol, fa, mi, re, do on "loo" or "la" from g^1. Repeat the procedure, moving the starting pitch upward by half-steps each time. Do the same exercise moving the starting pitch downward by half-steps with each repetition. Place the highest and lowest pitches students sing comfortably on the staff.

Matching Pitches: Play or sing each pitch and ask students to repeat them.

Tonal Memory: Play two or three short melodies and ask children to repeat them on "loo" or "la." These should be the same for all students.

Sight Reading: Select a short melody based on reading skills you or the music teacher have taught. Ask children to sing the melody using whatever system has been taught.

Singing Harmony: Select a two-part song children know well and ask them to sing the harmony as you sing the melody or vice versa.

Vocal Characteristics: Listen for tone color, resonance, volume, and pitch accuracy throughout the interview and make note of it here.

Name_____

Address_____

Phone_____

Homeroom_____

VOCAL INTERVIEW

1. Have you ever sung in a choir or singing group?_____

   If so,_____   _____

            where?   when?

2. Have you taken lessons on a musical instrument?_____

   _____   _____   _____

   What instrument?   How long have you   Who is your
                   taken lessons?   teacher?

3. Range:

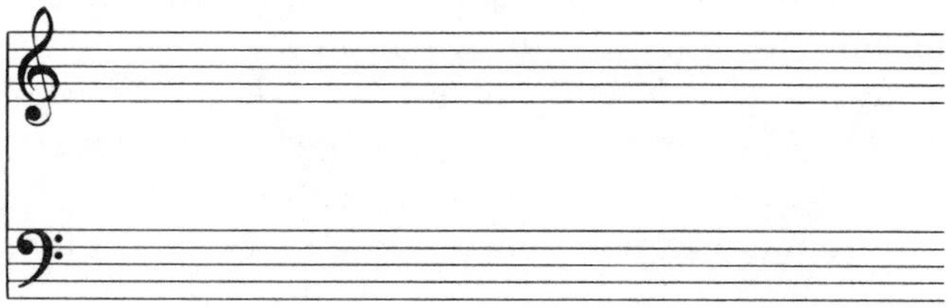

4. Pitch Matching: O G F N

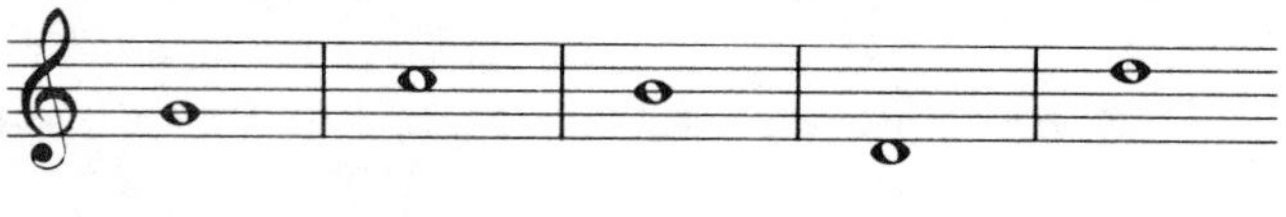

5. Tonal Memory: O G F N

6. Sight Reading: O G F N

7. Singing Harmony: O G F N

8. Vocal Characteristics:

9. Comments:

O = Outstanding   G = Good   F = Fair   N = Needs improvement

Figure 2–1

Comments: List any problems or strengths you hear.

As you listen to children sing, circle the appropriate letters (O G F N) to indicate their level of performance for each task. Add any additional comments at the bottom of the form to help remind you of particular vocal characteristics or problems children may have.

Group Evaluations

In situations where no time is available for individual assessments, a less detailed interview is desirable. A simpler interview form might be prepared that covers range, pitch accuracy, and a place for comments.

If possible, take a group of students to another area for their interview while a parent or administrator works with the remaining students. Students will usually be less self-conscious and perform better when they don't feel the rest of the chorus is listening to them.

Begin by having students sing a short familiar song together. Next ask them to sing the pattern sol, fa, mi, re, do on "loo" or "la" from g^1 downward. Repeat the procedure discussed earlier, asking students to drop out when tones become too high or too low. Note this on the student's interview form.

Next divide the group into two sections for singing a familiar two-part song. Give students an opportunity to sing both parts with the group and in smaller duets or quartets. Note how well students carry their part.

Throughout the interview you will need to listen for pitch accuracy and vocal characteristics as best you can. Obviously, it will be more difficult to clearly evaluate vocal skills in this setting, but it is possible and better than no evaluation at all.

THE UNDERDEVELOPED SINGER

With good vocal instruction in the primary grades, most normal children will sing with a fair degree of pitch accuracy by late third or fourth grade. It is not unusual, however, to find several students in a typical upper elementary class who consistently fail to sing on pitch. These children are underdeveloped singers and will, most likely, need remedial help.[2]

---

[2]Betty Richards Fischer, "The Under-developed Singer." *The Metronome*, Vol. 15, No. 1, (Fall 1978), p. 2.

Despite the notion that these children are "monotones" or "non-singers," with proper instruction they can almost always become adequate singers. According to Edwin Gordon, "It appears that, barring physical disability, anyone can learn to sing, just as anyone can learn to talk."[3]

Of course, there are levels of musical aptitude that affect singing skills and some children will achieve more readily than others. General intelligence affects one's ability to learn to sing just as it affects the learning of any skill. However, underdeveloped singers do not demonstrate an inability to learn to sing. In most cases, they simply have not had the tonal experiences necessary to develop accurate singing and are deficient in one or more of the following areas:

1. Receiving sensory impressions of tone,
2. Remembering these impressions and building a repertoire of tonal images,
3. Experimenting with and coordinating the voice and ear to imitate these sounds, or
4. Learning to compare vocal production with what is heard or remembered.

At this point, it will be helpful to look at various types of underdeveloped singers. In the elementary school these will most likely include (1) dependent singers, (2) speechlike singers, (3) limited-range singers, and (4) untuned singers.

The Dependent Singer

Dependent singers are those who sing on pitch in a group or with accompaniment, but fail to do so when they sing alone. Lack of experience singing alone and inattention to the task of singing are primary reasons for this problem. Usually these children are unaware of the control they have over their voices. They are accustomed to following others and often don't realize the added concentration and effort needed to sing accurately by oneself. This problem may be compounded by a fear of failure and/or a shy personality. Poor tonal memory and an inadequate sense of tonality may also contribute to the problem.

---

[3] Edwin Gordon, *The Psychology of Music Teaching*. Englewood Cliffs, NJ: Prentice-Hall, 1971, p. 93.

Because dependent singers are able to sing accurately with others, we know they are able to match pitches and have some degree of tonal memory. Most likely, these singers will benefit from short echoing exercises that will increase the tonal memory and provide opportunities for solo singing. The memorization of brief melodic patterns using sol-fa syllables is also helpful.

Dependent singers should be encouraged to sing "inside" their heads as well as with their voices. Learning to think or "image" a melody internally is an important skill needed for tuning the voice to create a given melody. This type of inner hearing requires a level of concentration most dependent singers are unfamiliar with. Therefore, encourage dependent singers to become actively responsible for developing their "inner" and "outer" voices.

Like all underdeveloped singers, dependent singers need many experiences singing and repeating tonal patterns. As these patterns are heard and performed over and over again, they become part of the child's tonal vocabulary. The extent of this tonal vocabulary will play an important part in the child's ability to reproduce melodies by him- or herself.

The Speechlike Singer

Speechlike singers have not discovered the difference between their speaking voice and their singing voice. Therefore, they attempt to sing just as they speak. There is little inflection in the voice and the range is usually limited to several pitches of the speaking voice.

In most cases, these children lack experience with vocal experimentation and have not learned to coordinate ear and voice for accurate vocal production. Often they have had little singing experience at home or in the primary school. Boys encounter this problem more often than girls, and this may be attributed, in part, to a desire to sound more masculine by using a deep voice. Furthermore, speechlike singers are usually unaware of the added energy and concentration needed to sing accurately.

Speechlike singers need many opportunities for vocal experimentation and imitation in order to feel and hear the difference between speaking and singing. Imitating the sounds of sirens, goblins, machines, and animals often helps to increase vocal flexibility. Exploring the whole gamut of vocal sounds from yells to whispers may be helpful as well. Glissandos are particularly useful in helping children move fluidly from low to high and vice versa. The use of physical gestures such as a swooping motion of the arm is also helpful.

In many cases, speechlike singers progress rapidly once they discover the sound and feel of their more flexible singing voice. This is because most are able to hear and remember tonal patterns, but have simply not learned how to produce the sounds vocally. Once the "new" voice is discovered, students may need to be reminded from time to time to use it in place of the old speechlike voice.

The Limited-Range Singer

As the name implies, limited-range singers are unable to sing in the normal expanded vocal range. This is most often demonstrated by students who sing in chest voice, but have not learned to sing in head voice. Others may consistently sing only a few notes in the mid or upper range.

Due to a lack of vocal experimentation and imitation, limited-range singers are unable to coordinate what they hear with what they produce vocally. Like most underdeveloped singers, they are usually unaware of the increased physical and mental energy necessary for accurate singing. In some cases, physical problems such as allergies or defects of the ear or throat may contribute significantly to the problem. Extreme emotional or physical tension can also play a part in limiting the vocal range.

Hearing, experimenting with, and imitating a wide variety of vocal sounds, as suggested for the speechlike singer, will also benefit the limited-range singer as long as physical problems are not a contributing factor.

Once the vocal range is expanded, some children will progress quickly and steadily toward accurate singing. It is likely, however, that a few students will need considerable remedial work at every level of tonal experience, beginning with the development of accurate pitch perception and the building of a tonal vocabulary. These students can be most challenging to work with because of their limited aural, as well as oral development.

The Untuned Singer

While all underdeveloped singers display some inability to sing in tune, untuned singers are defined as those who seem to lack any concept of tone matching. This may include students who sing in a normal vocal range, as well as former speechlike or limited-range singers who have expanded their range but still fail to match pitch accurately.

Untuned singers are usually deficient in several areas of tonal experience. In some cases, however, attention to singing may be all that is needed for vast improvement, thereby discovering the sound and feel of one's voice in unison with others. When this is the case, inexperience in singing and/or a lack of concentration are usually the contributing problems.

In more typical and complex cases, children may need work with pitch perception, building tonal memory and vocabulary, coordinating ear and voice for good vocal production, and learning to evaluate their vocal performance. In a sense, these students are musical infants and need careful and consistent nurturing if they are to become accurate singers. They are easily discouraged because they lack so many skills that may seem natural in other children.

Fortunately, this type of underdeveloped singer is rare, perhaps 3 percent to 5 percent in a typical elementary school. When working with these children, be sure to check school medical records to see if hearing loss is or has been a problem in the child's history. You are likely to find that children who are this severely underdeveloped have had some physical trauma, usually related to temporary or permanent hearing loss.

Working with the Underdeveloped Singer

No matter what the specific singing problems may be, most underdeveloped singers seem to benefit from a program of remedial instruction that uses a variety of tonal experiences with much emphasis on attentive listening. Beyond this, activities should be created or selected that will provide experiences more specifically needed by the individual child or group.

While the activities given here are listed in five categories, be aware that many of them can serve more than one purpose. For instance, all echoing activities are by nature listening and pitch-matching activities. Likewise, all activities suggested for building tonal memory are also good for developing attentive listening skills. This is because, while singing involves learning various skills, it is the integration of these skills that results in accurate vocal production.

Successful remedial instruction can take place on an individual basis or with a small group. A most important ingredient in either case seems to be the development of mutual trust between the students and teacher, and in groups, between the students themselves.

Short, but frequent sessions seem most successful. Weekly sessions of twenty to twenty-five minutes are appropriate for small groups, with shorter sessions twice a week particularly helpful for individual work. These short sessions might take place for five or ten minutes before or after school. Group sessions are most successful when they are scheduled as a music activity period during the school day. Work with your school administrator to include this time in your schedule.

Remember, if there has been a good program of vocal instruction throughout the elementary grades, the number of students needing remedial help should be few. Of course, this will vary in different areas and will be a greater problem in schools where the population is very transient.

When working with underdeveloped singers, use a wide variety of activities. Try to plan activities that will insure success. Avoid constant drill and be generous with words of encouragement. Be patient and don't expect miracles. For the 3 percent to 5 percent of children whose vocal skills are extremely underdeveloped, progress may seem slow and tedious. Never give up! Sometimes, seemingly out of the blue, these children can surprise you with a sudden surge of progress you never expected.

Suggestions and Activities for Developing Listening Skills

1. Explain to children that learning to listen carefully is essential to learning to sing. Developing good listening skills is the first step in developing a good singing voice.

2. Give children a pencil and paper and ask them to write every sound they hear within a 60-second period. When the time is up, have children share what they heard. Help children realize there are many sounds they hear every day that they don't notice until they listen carefully for them. This type of attentive, careful listening is needed for singing.

3. Tape record a variety of environmental sounds and ask children to identify them as they are played.

4. Underdeveloped singers are often unaware of the sound of their own voice. Make a recording of the child speaking and singing. Play the tape back allowing each child to hear his or her own voice.

5. Help children understand there are two types of hearing: hearing actual sounds with the "outer ears" and hearing imagined sounds with the "inner ears."

6. Ask children to list ten sounds they can hear with their "inner ears." These must be imagined sounds, not sounds they are actually hearing. For fun, have children imitate some of the sounds they imagined. Can others guess the sounds?

7. Tell children that good singers are like tape recorders. They must be able to receive, record, and replay in order to sing accurately. For singers the ears are the receiver, the mind is the recorder, and the voice is responsible for replaying. If any part is not functioning properly, the sound will be distorted.

8. Play echoing games using these "human recorders." Children enjoy echoing spooky sounds, animal sounds, silly sentences, and simple short phrases in foreign languages.

9. Play listening games in which children must identify characteristics of sound such as (a) high or low, (b) upward or downward movement, and (c) melodic movement by skip or step.

10. A particularly effective listening game begins by asking a child to sing any pitch he or she chooses. Respond by singing a pitch that is the same or different. Using the words higher, lower, or the same, ask the child to tell which word best describes your response to his or her pitch.

11. More suggestions for developing listening skills can be found in Chapter 3.

Suggestions and Activities for Developing Pitch-Matching

1. First activities in pitch-matching should begin in the range where the student is most comfortable. Most often this is in the range of middle c^1 to g^1, but be sure to investigate with each child to discover where he or she feels the most secure.

2. To help children better hear their own voices as they respond in pitch-matching activities, ask them to gently cup their hands behind their ears.

3. Pitch-matching requires an awareness of the sound and feel of oneness of tone created by unison singing. To help a child experience the sensation of unison, ask him or her to sing a pitch and to sustain it as you match the pitch with your voice or play a note on the piano and sing it with the child to create unison. At another time, make a tape recording of the child singing different pitches in his or her range. Replay the tape and ask the child to match his or her own pitches.

4. To comprehend unison, it is helpful to hear what unison is not. Play a pitch on the piano and match it in unison or sing another pitch. Ask the child if your pitch is the same as or different from the pitch played on the piano.

5. It is very important that children think (image) a pitch before they actually sing it. Humming seems to help children image the pitch just before it is sounded. Once children can produce the pitch on a hum, have them open to a "mah" sound sustaining the same pitch.

6. The echoing activities already suggested in this chapter are also good exercises for improving pitch accuracy. Remember when using such activities that melodies that move by skip are usually easier to sing than melodies that move by step. Melodies that use the descending minor third and other intervals of the pentatonic scale are especially good for underdeveloped singers.

7. Pitch-matching activities should be varied and should include, as soon as possible, the singing of songs or phrases of songs. Always use familiar melodies and, preferably, those the children choose. Pitch melodies in the most comfortable range possible for the singers. Songs with a narrow vocal range and repetitious melody are usually best. Some good beginning tunes include: "Rain Rain Go Away," "Hot Cross Buns," "Jingle Bells," "Marching to Pretoria," and "Mary Had a Little Lamb."

8. Several years ago, I came across Marian Flagg's four-step process for developing vocal accuracy. (See *Music Learning* by Marian Flagg. Boston: C. C. Birchard and Co., 1949.) It has been an invaluable tool for working with many underdeveloped singers since. While actually nothing more than an echoing exercise between student and teacher, dividing it into four distinct parts seems to sharpen the child's ability to hear and reproduce the sound.

First the teacher sings a pitch within the child's singing range. The child is asked to: (a) hear it outside, (b) hear it inside, (c) sing it, and (d) decide if he or she is right or wrong.

Suggestions and Activities for Developing Tonal Memory

1. The use of melody bells is often helpful for children who have poor tonal memory. Begin by using only two or three pitches within the child's vocal range. Sing and play a melody such as g^1–e^1–g^1. Allow an appropriate number of silent beats for children to image the tune internally. Then have them echo the tune on the bells and with their voices. (In early sessions the singing responses will probably be inaccurate. Don't be overly concerned about this.)

2. Once children are familiar with this bell activity, let them "call" the melodies. It is helpful to limit the number of different tones and beats used for each exercise. Too many different pitches confuse

children and make the melodies difficult to remember. Also, avoid the use of chromatics and awkward leaps.

For each session using this activity, concentrate on a limited number of pitches and intervals. For instance, one day all melodies might use only the tones c^1, e^1, and g^1.

3. Sing short melodic patterns within the child's vocal range and ask the child to echo what he or she hears. Expand the number of beats and intervals only when the child is comfortable with the initial patterns.

4. Sing two tones and allow enough time for the child to hear them in his or her "inner ear." Ask the child to respond with the words "same" or "different." Make the game more challenging by singing intervals and short melodic phrases.

5. Visual aids are often helpful in developing tonal memory. Use lines, dots, or a series of notes to illustrate several different melodies. Play melodies that go with each illustration. Next, play one of the melodies at random and see if the child can match it to the correct illustration.

6. Sing a three-beat melody and allow three beats for the child to image the melody in his or her mind. Have the child draw the shape of the melody on the board or in the air with his or her arms.

7. Have children memorize short melodic patterns like sol–mi, sol–la–sol–mi, sol–mi–do, do–mi–sol, and do^1–sol–la–ti–do^1. Have children record them on tape and practice them with the tape at home.

8. The sequence of instruction found in the Kodály approach is excellent for building tonal memory. Most books based on this approach contain many games, activities, and songs that can be used successfully with underdeveloped singers. If you are unfamiliar with the Kodály approach, an address for the Organization of American Kodály Educators can be found in Chapter 9.

9. Encourage children to practice pitch-matching daily by assigning homework such as (a) listening to and echoing pitches, intervals, or sol–fa melodies from a tape recording, (b) if a child has a piano, ask him or her to practice matching pitches within his or her range at the keyboard, and (c) tape-record songs and encourage children to play them and sing along at home.

Suggestions and Activities for Finding the Singing Voice

1. Demonstrate the difference between the speaking and singing voices for your students. Tell children that all people have both types of voices and that all people can learn to sing just as they can learn to

speak. Lead children to discover that the singing voice is more flexible and feels lighter, yet it takes more energy and air to sing.

2. Ask children to identify the differences between speaking and singing voices. Some of these might include:

Speaking	*Singing*
lower	higher
darker	brighter
fewer tones	more different tones
choppier	smoother

3. Ask children to listen as you sing or speak short phrases. Following each phrase, ask children to respond with the word "speaking" or "singing."

4. Play a tape recording of different people speaking or singing. If possible include familiar people children know, like the school secretary or principal. Ask these people to demonstrate the difference in their speaking and singing voices. Also, use popular recordings where singers speak while music is played in the background.

5. Lead children in the echoes (a) "This is a speaking voice" (spoken), and (b) "This is a singing voice" (sung).

6. Helen Kemp, formerly of Westminster Choir College, suggests that children think of singing and speaking as two different "channels." To sing, children must tune their voices to their "singing channel." This "channel" has a lighter, brighter sound and feel than the speaking channel.

7. Help children understand that for singing: (a) deep breathing is necessary, (b) the mouth and throat must open, (c) the body should feel buoyant, and (d) the mind must be attentive to what is being sung. Speechlike singers often fail to do one or more of these when they attempt to sing.

Suggestions and Activities for Expanding Vocal Range

1. Ask children to echo whatever you say or do. Use dramatic sentences, repeating them and varying pitch and inflection each time. For instance:

> *Don't* eat little brown worms.
> Don't *eat* little brown worms (and so on).

2. Expand this activity to include other vocalizations, such as laughing, crying, yelling, and whispering. Use your own voice dramatically, varying pitch and inflection.

3. The following sounds used as echoes are particularly good for "freeing" the voice: (a) the "hoo" of an owl, (b) sounds of sirens, (c) sounds of ghosts and goblins, (d) the "caw-caw" call of a crow, and (e) the "beep-beep" of TV's roadrunner.

4. As children become comfortable with echoing activities, begin to include simple chants that vary in pitch. The patterns sol–mi and sol–la–sol–mi are especially good for starters. Include occasional rhythmic patterns and environmental sounds such as tapping or scraping to add variety.

5. Use glissandos to encourage vocal flexibility. Draw imaginary rollercoaster or elevator rides in the air or on the chalkboard to help children feel and visualize the movement of the sound.

6. Play "The Lost Mountain Climber" game. Stand on a chair at one end of the room with the child or a small group of children at the other end on chairs also. Pretend you are calling for help, but all you hear is your echo. Basic patterns using sol, mi, and la work well. Vary the game by having a student call for help while you become the echo.

7. Do a similar activity by pretending you are a parent calling your child to come home for dinner. Improvise a humorous conversation as the child makes excuses for not being able to come home.

8. For children who initially can produce only two or three pitches, begin echo activities by echoing the child's pitch. Make up echoes or a conversation using these pitches. Gradually introduce other pitches.

9. Children who consistently sing above the appropriate pitch will benefit from attention to breathing and using more energy for singing. Glissandos that move in a downward direction are particularly helpful.

10. For children who sing accurately in chest voice but have not developed head voice, see Chapter 3.

Throughout all of the activities suggested here, your attitude is of utmost importance. Underdeveloped singers are usually painfully aware of their inability to sing like most other students. Therefore, you must not only be knowledgeable, but accepting and encouraging as well if students are to overcome their fears and reach their fullest potential.

Underdeveloped singers are ready to "graduate" from remedial instruction when they can match pitches in a normal expanded vocal range and can sing simple tunes accurately with little or no help. Graduates should be reminded they will continually need to concentrate on and practice their new singing skills.

SECTION TWO

DEVELOPING A FINE CHILDREN'S CHOIR

Knowledge of fundamentals is prerequisite to free flight.

Robert Shaw

Chapter 3
Foundations of Good Choral Singing

THE ROLE OF THE CHORAL TEACHER

The knowledge and skills of the choral teacher are the two most important factors in developing a good children's choir. If the teacher is knowledgeable and able to communicate effectively with young singers, a good choral sound is a likely result. Even the most unlikely and untalented group of youngsters can do marvelous things in the hands of an informed and interested teacher. More specifically, to achieve the best choral sound with an elementary school chorus, the choral teacher should have (1) a basic understanding of the child voice, (2) a basic understanding of vocal techniques, (3) some knowledge and skill in choral conducting, and (4) a love of children and singing. With the exception of number four, this book can help you in each of these areas.

Developing a Sound Ideal

Another basic responsibility of the choral teacher is the development of a "sound ideal" for the chorus. This ideal is an imagined sound the choral teacher holds in his or her mind. It represents how the chorus will sound when its potential is reached. The transference of this "sound ideal" from the choral teacher to the students is essential for the development of a good choral sound.

To effectively develop and teach your own "sound ideal" it will be helpful to (a) become acquainted with the characteristics of fine children's choirs, (b) listen to outstanding children's choirs, (c) assess, as best you can, the potential of your chorus, (d) learn techniques for communicating your "sound ideal" to your students, and (e) develop your own listening skills.

Characteristics of Fine Children's Choirs

Most fine children's choirs will have the following characteristics in common:

1. The use of head voice provides an overall light and forward tone.
2. There is no apparent breathiness of tone. Children breathe silently and in appropriate places to create expressive phrasing and a smooth vocal line.
3. Diction is clear. Words are understandable because consonants are clear and vowels are uniformly shaped.
4. The overall tone is unique from that of an adult or adolescent choir. There is no vibrato, harshness, or pinching of the tone.
5. Individual voices are blended so that no single voice is heard above others.
6. Intonation is accurate.
7. There is a combination of unison and part singing.
8. Some à cappella singing is generally a part of the repertoire.
9. The singing is expressive and conveys the mood and meaning of the words.
10. The director's conducting is expressive and precise. Children are attentive and responsive to the director.

Listening to Children's Choirs

While becoming acquainted with the characteristics of a good children's choir is helpful, there is no substitute for actually listening to fine performances. Outstanding children's choirs often perform as part of Music Educator's Conferences, The American Choral Directors Association Programs, Choristers Guild Festivals, and workshops presented by Kodály and Orff educators. Investigate to see when these organizations may be sponsoring children's choral performances in your state or area. You will find the addresses of these organizations in Chapter 9.

Recordings are another way of listening to fine children's choirs. The following are by three outstanding choirs and can be ordered at the addresses given here:

Singing the Seasons of the Lord
  by the Mennonite Children's Choir
  Choristers Guild
  P.O. Box 802
  Dayton, OH 45401

The Glen Ellyn Children's Chorus
  directed by Doreen Rao
  Glen Ellyn Park District
  671 Crescent Blvd.
  Glen Ellyn, IL 60137

With Joyful Hearts and Voices
  by the Westwood Choristers
  Augsburg Publishing House
  426 S. 5th Street
  Box 1209
  Minneapolis, MN 55440

Great Hymns for Children
  (also by the Westwood Choristers)

Unfortunately, the recordings of one of the finest American Children's Choirs, The Carillon Choristers, under the direction of Edith Norberg, are no longer available from Augsburg Publishing House. However, it would be worth the effort of any interested choral teacher to try to obtain these recordings through a library.

Assessing Your Choir's Potential

Most often teachers underestimate the ability of their students. If a child does not sing beautifully, we may assume he never will. To the contrary, children who seem to have rather average voices may have the potential to sing beautifully with proper instruction. Children who have never sung in head voice may be able to create light, floating tones easily when encouraged by a knowledgeable teacher. A child who is unsure of pitch may develop pitch security after only a short time in an organized singing program.

Intelligence is an important factor in determining singing potential. Often times children who are not necessarily skilled singers, but who have good native intelligence, learn to sing easily just as they learn other skills. They are able to synthesize the components of good singing and to concentrate on achieving an appropriate sound.

The emotional characteristics of students are also factors in determining their potential. Children who are happy, interested, and have a basically positive outlook on life, tend to be more successful chorus members. Of course, there are exceptions to this notion.

Sometimes a very fine young singer may not be particularly emotionally or socially well adjusted. The important ingredient here seems to be a sensitivity to life and the ability to feel and express the meaning and mood of the music. Occasionally, these students will excel in chorus while they do poorly in most other areas.

If you have a high percentage of chorus members who play musical instruments, chances are your chorus will progress more rapidly when learning singing skills. Students who study a musical instrument are usually good music readers. Good readers make learning music more efficient and, in turn, allow more time for refining singing skills.

Beyond the skills and talents of your students, the amount and quality of time you spend with them will be significant factors in determining what they will achieve. No matter how talented they are, if you see them once a week for fifteen minutes, it will be impossible for them to develop their full potential. Time must be taken into consideration as you try to set realistic expectations for your chorus.

Assessing your group's potential is a subjective judgment at best. No matter what your initial impressions may be, be ready to alter your expectations. The most unlikely group of singers may surprise you with their eagerness to learn and their love of performing. On the other hand, a group of rather talented students may disappoint you by their lack of interest or unwillingness to give their best.

Whatever the case may be, assess your students' potential as honestly as possible. Then, challenge them to do their best!

Communicating a Sound Ideal

Through listening to fine children's choirs, it is possible to develop a standard of excellence. However, this standard may be far beyond the ability of your singers. For this reason, it is important that the choral teacher establish a "sound ideal" that incorporates the students' potential as well as a high standard of excellence. This is not to say that you should not have high standards. However, it is to say that children will have greater success when goals are realistic and attainable.

The Teacher as Model

Because imitation is such a basic part of learning to sing, it is important that children have a good singing model. Ideally, this model will be the choral teacher. The teacher who is able to demonstrate the sound he or she is after is at a distinct advantage. For this reason, it would be a great benefit both for anyone directing a children's choir and the students if he or she were to take some type of voice instruction.

If you have had little or no voice training, approach a reputable voice teacher and explain your situation. You may be surprised at all you can learn in a few short lessons or classes. Remember, your goal need not be the Metropolitan Opera but simply gaining enough confidence in your own singing ability to provide an effective model for your students.

Qualities of a Good Singing Model

The ideal sound of the child voice is not that of an adult. Therefore, the teacher, or whoever is used as a vocal model should be able to demonstrate in the following manner:

1. The singing voice should be light and clear. Vibrato should be avoided as well as the use of chest voice. For adult male singers, the use of a light falsetto is most desirable.
2. Intonation should be accurate.
3. The model should be able to demonstrate nuances of dynamics, tone color, and expression.
4. When demonstrating aspects of diction, the model should be able to accurately enunciate vowels and clearly articulate consonants.
5. The singing voice should be free of scooping or pushing at the beginning of words.
6. If the singing model is visual as well as aural, good posture and facial expressions are important.

The Effective Use of Modeling

While modeling can be an important help in building a good choral sound, it should be used sparingly, interspersed in the rehearsal at points where specific problems occur. Demonstrations should be short and to the point allowing the vast majority of rehearsal time to be spent with children singing—not the teacher. As a rule of thumb, never stop children from singing to demonstrate something unless they are given the opportunity to re-create the demonstration themselves. Modeling may be particularly effective in the following situations:

1. Demonstrating a particular vowel sound needed on a certain word,

2. Helping children hear and feel the expression needed in a vocal line,

3. Providing a model of crisp articulation,

4. Letting children hear a desired tone color, or

5. Demonstrating a needed correction in pitch, rhythm, or intonation.

Sometimes it is helpful for the teacher to imitate the sound he or she hears from the students. Children are often unaware of the sounds they sing. If the teacher can appropriately re-create the sound for the students and help them improve the sound, imitation can be helpful. The teacher should be very careful, however, never to make fun of the students' sound and always to offer a suggestion for ways to improve it.

Alternatives to the Teacher as Model

It is quite possible for teachers with little vocal training to achieve a good choral sound and good vocal instruction for their students. As long as the teacher has an appropriate "sound ideal" in his or her own mind and if he or she is able to communicate how to achieve this to the students, the result will most likely be a good choral sound.

If you are uncomfortable demonstrating for your students, the following suggestions may be helpful:

1. Select several of your better students at the beginning of the year to be your "singing assistants." Let them know you will be calling on them from time to time to demonstrate for other members of the chorus. Most children consider this quite an honor and are pleased to assist.

2. Ask singers from the community to demonstrate from time to time.

3. Use recordings of outstanding children's choirs to help children hear the sound you are after.

4. Invite a capable parent, teacher, or high school student to come to rehearsals or to make demonstration tapes for you.

5. From the start, let children know you would like them to sing individually on occasion. During rehearsal, if you hear a child performing particularly well, ask him or her to sing for the rest of the group. Follow this by allowing the group to imitate the example. It is important with youngsters, however, that you are sure the child will not be embarrassed by this. Only ask a child to demonstrate when you are

sure he or she will feel comfortable doing so. In general, fostering an attitude of acceptance throughout rehearsals will help to make children less fearful of modeling individually.

6. Remember, your knowledge and enthusiasm for singing are far more important than your ability as a solo singer. Good diction, intonation, rhythmic accuracy, breathing, posture, and expression can all be demonstrated effectively by you, even if you don't regard yourself as a fine singer.

Other Ways of Communicating the Sound Ideal

While modeling can be a helpful tool in building a good choral sound, the teacher's ability to communicate his or her sound ideal can also be accomplished in other ways. Not every winning baseball coach is able to hit and field as well as the players; however, the coach must be able to communicate to them how they can improve their own skills. The same is true for a good choral teacher. Communicating your knowledge to your singers effectively may include the following:

1. Set high standards from the very beginning. Let your students know you will accept nothing but their best.

2. Use facial expressions and your conducting skills to relate desired change. The more you are able to communicate without stopping the music, the more efficient your rehearsals will be.

3. Make suggestions quickly and to the point. Lengthy explanations are boring and will break the momentum of your rehearsal. A single word such as "legato" may be all that is necessary to achieve a desired change.

4. Think of as many reasons as possible to rehearse a particular musical phrase or section. Rehearse it for diction, phrasing, tone color, intonation, blend, and balance. Each time you rehearse the phrase, have specific goals in mind. Share these with students so they know why they're repeating it.

5. Use illustrations from pieces of music already learned. For instance, if your chorus learned to use staggered breathing in a Christmas song, remind them of how this was done when they encounter an especially long phrase in a new piece.

6. When a problem arises, ask children how it might be solved. For instance, if you hear too much "r" in the word Lord, tell children what you hear and ask them how it should be corrected.

7. Use every rehearsal and all the music you sing as building blocks of experience and knowledge for your young singers. If you do so, you will not need to reteach basics each time you rehearse.

8. Let students know you expect them to be responsible for applying what they have learned to new situations. Tell them you will share with them all the knowledge you can, but in the end they must become responsible for improving their singing skills. The best singers are those who are able to anticipate the teacher's suggestions, without being told.

9. No matter how high your standards may be, always try to foster an attitude of acceptance and trust. If children sense that you sincerely care about them, they will trust you. If they trust you, they will be responsive to your suggestions. If they are responsive to your suggestions, a good choral sound is likely to result.

Improving Your Listening Skills

One of the most important jobs of the choral teacher is to be an attentive listener. This listening should be directed at the overall sound of the chorus as well as at the particulars of tone color, pitch, diction, balance, blend, and phrasing. It is only through careful listening that the teacher is able to identify what specific sounds need improvement. As particular problems are identified and worked on, the overall choral sound is improved.

To improve your own listening skills, try some of the following suggestions:

1. Rehearse without accompaniment whenever possible. Too often the piano can cover a multitude of problems.

2. If at all possible, do not accompany your chorus yourself. There is much a choral director has to think about and listen for without being tied to the keyboard.

3. Close your eyes and listen to your chorus (of course, explain what you are doing first). It is amazing how much more critical the ear becomes without visual distraction.

4. From time to time, place special attention on one aspect of the music you're studying. For instance, emphasize tall, carefully shaped vowel sounds for one rehearsal. Focus your listening attention on this aspect of the music.

5. Rehearse one section or a smaller group of children from time to time. Focus your attention on the individual vocal problems children

may be having. Sometimes a section will perform something incorrectly that slips by when performed with the whole group. Learn to listen for parts as well as the overall effect.

6. Avoid singing with your children in rehearsal and performance. Sometimes directors sing so they can avoid hearing problems children are having. Demonstration is important, but once children begin to sing, let them do so independently.

7. Move about the rehearsal area listening for individual voices. You may find that an intonation or diction problem stems from one person or a few individuals. You can save much time and energy by working with these students individually or in small groups.

8. Occasionally, try to listen as if you have never heard a particular piece of music before. Imagine yourself as someone in the audience who knows nothing of the intricacies that have been so carefully worked out in the music. What is the overall effect of the sound?

9. Occasionally, hold rehearsals in different rooms or settings. Listen carefully for the subtle and not so subtle changes that occur when the performance area is changed.

10. Once you have rehearsed a certain aspect of a piece of music, do not assume it will be performed correctly from that time on. Children may forget something that has been worked out to perfection at one time. Keep your ears alert for what is actually being sung.

11. Record and listen to a tape of your children singing. Use your ears to pinpoint problems that need attention.

12. As you rehearse, ask yourself these four questions:

- Are rhythms and pitches accurate?
- Is the tone pleasing?
- Are the words clear and understandable?
- Is the music expressive?

TEACHING CHILDREN TO LISTEN

> If the director uses his ears, the greatest gift he can confer upon his choir and its audience is to teach them to do the same.[1]

Most normal children can hear, but few are good listeners. Good listeners are able to focus on one aspect of an aural experience. In the singing situation, they are able to hear themselves as well as others.

---

[1] Ruth Krehbiel Jacobs, *The Successful Children's Choir.* Chicago, IL: H. T. Fitzsimons Co., Inc., 1948, p. 43.

They can discriminate between appropriate and inappropriate singing sounds. They seem to have a well-developed sense of pitch and are able to evaluate and correct their own performance.

Good singers are good listeners and just as children can learn to sing, they can also learn the skill of careful listening. The first step in this process is building an awareness of the importance of listening. Next, through the transference of the choral teacher's "sound ideal," students should begin to develop a standard by which they can evaluate what they hear. Finally, the overall sound is affected as children make modifications in their singing, based on what they hear.

Suggestions for Teaching Listening Skills

1. To draw children's attention to the importance of listening, teach them "The Listening Song" (see Figure 3–1). Use the song as a warm-up from time to time.

Figure 3–1

("The Listening Song" can be sung as a round.)

2. Tell children that good singers use their ears as well as their voices when they sing. Use the phrase "sing with your ears" to help focus attention on listening.

3. From time to time ask students to sing very lightly. As they sing, ask them to listen to the voices around them. This is particularly helpful in warm-up exercises.

4. Purchase the following posters for your rehearsal area:

"Singing Is Listening" from Popplers Music Store, 123 Demers Avenue, P.O. Box 398, Grand Forks, ND 58201.

"Is Your Mouth in Motion Before Your Ears Are in Gear?" from Choristers Guild, 501 East Third Street, P.O. Box 802, Dayton, OH 45401.

5. Do vocal echoes with your chorus. Sing a pitch and wait about three seconds before cueing the children to respond. The first two seconds give children time to hear and think the pitches inside their heads. The final second allows time for a breath. Some children will want to sing immediately after you. Encourage them to wait a few seconds so they will be more prepared to sing accurately.

6. Emphasize the importance of "thinking" what you are going to sing before you sing it. Of course, this is actually a way of developing inner hearing that is so important in any singing experience. Put the words THINK—BREATHE—SING[2] someplace in front of the rehearsal area. As children learn to use this in their singing, they are learning to "hear" before they actually begin to sing.

7. Further develop inner hearing by playing the "radio game." Set the tempo and give students the starting pitch for a familiar song. Pretend you are pushing an "on-off" button on a radio. When you push the "off" button, children should stop singing aloud but continue "singing" the tune in their heads. When you push the "on" button the singing should resume.

8. Devote a small part of each rehearsal to ear training using solfège. Use Kodály (Curwen) hand signs to lead singing or have children read notation from their music or the chalk board. Using solfège is an important key to building good intonation and tonal relationships.

9. Ask children to write short poems about the importance of listening in singing. Post these in the chorus room, or select one or two

---

[2] John Yarrington, *Sound Recipes for Teenage Voices.* Dallas: Choristers Guild, 1980, p. 14.

of the best, write them out on poster board, and put them some place in the rehearsal area. Here is an example:

> If my ears forget to listen, as my
> voice begins to sing—
> I should probably be quiet
> and never sing a thing!

10. Tape-record a segment of a song as children sing. As you play the tape, ask children to listen for what needs improvement. List problem areas on the chalkboard and then ask students to suggest ways to correct the problems. Re-record the same music and listen to see if the problems are corrected.

11. When you are rehearsing one voice part (soprano, second soprano, or alto) ask students who are not singing to listen for something specific. Questions like, "Are the vowel sounds uniform?" and "Describe the tone color you hear" help to focus listening.

12. Record a rehearsal or performance and ask children to listen and critique the performance. A form might be made up with questions like, "What piece do you feel sounded the best?" "Why?" "In which piece did we sing under pitch?" "What would you suggest to correct this?"

THE IMPORTANCE OF HEAD VOICE

If a children's choir is to have a beautiful singing tone, emphasis must be placed on developing the head voice (sometimes referred to as head register). The light forward tone produced when singing in this register not only results in a beautiful sound but it also helps to extend the child's vocal range and to give greater flexibility to the voice.

Most upper elementary age children are able to sing in two registers. These registers are usually defined as a series of tones produced by the same vocal mechanism and encompassing the following tones:

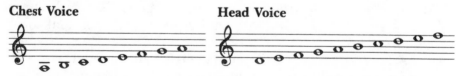

Chest Voice   **Head Voice**

At first glance it may appear that the difference in these voices or registers is merely one of range; chest voice encompassing the lower tones of the voice and head voice the upper tones. However, the overlapping tones from about d^1 to a^1 in the middle voice help to point up the fact that head voice and chest voice are not simply two different ranges.

The quality of tone produced in this middle area of the voice will be greatly affected by the register the child sings in. If chest voice is emphasized here, the tone may become harsh and heavy. As the child approaches the tones of a^1, b^1, and c^2, there may be an abrupt break in the voice as he or she tries to force chest tones into this area. On the other hand, if the child is encouraged to develop the head voice to its fullest, he or she will learn to extend the lighter tones into this middle range. The voice break around a^1, b^1, and c^2 will be avoided and the overall consistency of tone will be enhanced. As a general rule, for beauty of tone and greater flexibility, extend the head voice downward through the tones of this middle range.

How can you tell if your students are singing in head voice or chest voice? Here are some tips that will help you decide.

Chest Voice	*Head Voice*
1. Tone may be heavy, dark or shouty.	1. Tone is light and forward.
2. Child may appear to tense up as he or she reaches upper middle tones.	2. Child is relaxed and tones flow easily with little tension.
3. Child may raise the chin or stretch the neck when approaching higher tones.	3. Child is able to sing higher tones comfortably without lifting the chin.
4. There will be a noticeable change in tone quality as the child sings upward at about b^1 or c^2.	4. There is no distinct change in tone quality as the child moves from mid-voice to upper voice.
5. This voice is often used for recreational singing and can be very loud and raucous.	5. This is the voice primarily used by fine children's choirs.

Obviously from the lists given here, it is important to emphasize the use of head voice if the children's choir is to produce the best tone possible. This is not to say that there is never a time when chest voice is appropriate. The use of this voice should be limited, however, and should be exercised carefully to insure an appropriate singing sound.

Unfortunately, many of the singing models children have use chest voice exclusively. This is particularly true of popular female singers. Most adults who have had little vocal training will tend to use their chest voice. Children are often comfortable using this voice because it more closely approximates their speaking voice.

Therefore, the teacher of the children's choir must be prepared with activities and ideas that will help children develop the comfortable use of head voice. The results will be well worth the effort.

Characteristics of a Choir with Well-Developed Head Voice

1. Light, forward tone.
2. Expanded range in upper tones.
3. Can sing more difficult music because of increased range and flexibility.
4. Can carry head voice downward to about d^1.
5. There is no abrupt break between the chest and head voice.

Activities to Help Children Develop Head Voice

1. Demonstrate the break between chest voice and head voice for children by singing from middle c^1 to about e^2. Sing full voice and ask children to raise their hands when they hear a distinct change in the sound of your voice. Explain that you have moved from chest voice into head voice.

2. Have children do the same exercise. Have them raise their hands when they feel the change in their voices. (Some children with naturally light voices may not experience this sensation. This is good. Tell them not to be concerned, they're ahead of the game.)

3. After you have done the exercise mentioned above, emphasize the importance of moving smoothly from one register to the other. Point out that the best singers are those who are able to sing over this point with no break. This can be done by learning to sing lightly in chest voice and by learning to carry the head voice down as far as possible.

4. Use descending vocalises starting at about d^2. Since this begins well into the head voice range, ask children to carry the forward sensation of head voice downward. Choose one of the following exercises and repeat it several times, moving upward or downward by half steps with each repetition:

5. To extend the upper range of the head voice, use any of the previous exercises starting each new series a half-step higher.

6. Observe the facial expressions of your children as they sing. If you see students who appear to be straining on pitches above a^1, arrange a time to work with them individually. Chances are they are trying to carry chest voice into the head voice range.

7. Discuss with children the wide variety of sounds the human voice can make. Make a list of these and experiment with the different sounds. Here are a few:

whisper	cry
yell	laugh
speak	hum
sing	buzz

8. Focus on these three aspects of the voice: speaking, yelling, singing. How do they differ? How are they alike?

9. Ask children to put one hand on their chest as they loudly say the words, "My country 'tis of thee." Ask, "What do you feel?" Most children will sense a vibration in the chest area. Repeat this procedure asking children to sing the phrase starting on d^1. This time most children will feel the vibration diminish a little. Finally, ask children to sing the phrase lightly, starting on b^1. At this point children will most likely tell you they feel no vibration in the chest. This is a sure-fire experiment to help children feel and understand the difference between the speaking voice, chest voice, and head voice.

10. To help children "find" and use their head voices, suggest the following:

"Make the sound come from the front of your forehead instead of your chest."

"When you sing, feel as if you are yawning. Arch the roof of your mouth." (Soft palate.)

"Let the tones float."

"Think the tones in your head, not in your chest or throat."

"Sing from behind your eyes."

11. Play the song "Tomorrow" from the Broadway show, *Annie*, and "Who Will Buy?" from the movie version of *Oliver*. Lead children to discover that Annie sings in chest voice while Oliver uses head voice. Explain to children that young actresses and actors have much vocal training and that using the voice as Annie does is very hard on the voice. Children who get parts in plays like this are very exceptional. Most children would become hoarse after singing like this for any period of time.

12. Sometimes boys who have had little singing experience think singing in head voice is for girls only. Work with these boys individually and point out that boys and girls both need to develop head voice. Discuss voice change with the boys and help them understand that the more they develop their head voices now, the better control they will have when their voices change and the better their voices will be after they change. Some of the finest male singers in the world were once boy sopranos.

13. Further encourage boys to use head voice by having a "boys only" rehearsal. Invite male high school or college students to the rehearsal to demonstrate the qualities of the bass and tenor voice. Tell your guests ahead of time that you want to emphasize the importance of using head voice before voice change. A few words of encouragement from these "mature" singers may be a big help in teaching the importance of head voice to your boys.

14. Use a variety of "silly sounds" to build flexibility between head and chest voice. These may include echoes of sirens, hooting, ghost sounds, and sliding from pitch to pitch.

DEVELOPING GOOD SINGING POSTURE

There is no question that good, alert posture is necessary for good singing. In our society the virtues of good posture are, unfortunately, seldom stressed and most students have no idea of what we mean by "correct singing posture."

For rehearsals or performances when students are seated, the following guidelines should be followed:

1. Sit away from the back of the chair.

2. Place feet flat on the floor.

3. The back is straight and the head feels as if it is suspended from the ceiling by a string attached to the crown of the head.

4. The chest is held high while the chin is down.

The same principles apply when students are standing:

1. The spine is straight with the chest held high.
2. Feet are slightly apart with one foot a few inches ahead of the other.
3. The balance of body weight is slightly forward.
4. Arms are relaxed and held comfortably at the sides.

If students are using music, it should be held at about chest height, not in front of their faces or in their laps. Holding music at this level makes it easy for children to glance at their music when necessary. If music is held too high or too low, it will not only interrupt eye contact with the director, but it will also distort and diminish the tone.

Of course, the type of posture mentioned here should not be maintained throughout an entire rehearsal. Children are very active creatures and need to vary their body positions frequently. As a rule of thumb, it is a good idea to require "singing posture" just before students begin to sing and to continue until the director's final cut-off. Between songs or while another section is being rehearsed, allow children to sit back and relax. Be careful though—sometimes this may be interpreted as "time off" or time to talk. Be sure students know they are still expected to pay attention to the work at hand.

If you also work with your chorus members in general music, this type of attention to posture should begin at about fourth grade. When students come to chorus the foundations of good singing posture will already be established. If you only see your students during chorus, however, begin the very first rehearsal with attention to posture. Within a few short rehearsals, correct singing posture should become second nature to your students.

Suggestions for Teaching Good Singing Posture

1. Begin by helping students to think of their entire bodies as musical instruments. Just as a flutist or cellist must learn to hold his instrument correctly, the singer must do the same.

2. Have several instrumental students demonstrate what happens when they hold their instruments incorrectly. Experiment with what happens when singers hold their instruments incorrectly. How does it affect the sound?

3. Students often grasp the concept of good posture when an analogy is made with a garden hose. What happens when the hose is bent? What happens when it is straight? The same principle holds true

for singers. Sloppy posture interferes with the flow of air through the windpipe and can diminish the sound produced.

4. Some students better understand the importance of good posture when it is compared to the stance or posture needed in certain sports. Have several athletic students demonstrate the correct posture for their sports. Baseball batters, golfers, and gymnasts are particularly good examples.

5. Offer positive reinforcement to students who demonstrate good posture. "Bill's singing posture is absolutely perfect." "I noticed during the last number that everyone in the second row of altos had perfect posture." You need to be constantly aware of good posture and your students need to know that you are.

6. For children who tend to slouch:

a. Have them pretend their spines are as straight as yardsticks.

b. Ask students to clasp their hands behind their backs. This will automatically bring the chest up and prevent the shoulders from drooping. Ask students to release their hands slowly, keeping the chest and shoulders in correct position.

7. Take photographs of students who demonstrate correct singing posture. Better yet, invite a school administrator or parent to take the photos during an actual rehearsal. When the photographer arrives, have students describe the type of posture they should look for. To avoid confusion during the rehearsal, be sure to explain to students what will be happening ahead of time. Use the finished photos for a bulletin board display.

8. Ask several artistically talented students to submit sketches of students using good singing posture. Select the sketch you think most clearly illustrates all the aspects of good posture. Ask the students to do a life-size drawing to be displayed in the chorus room.

9. Sponsor a poster contest about good singing posture. Display the winning entries around the music room or in the hall.

10. Teach the "Posture Warm-Up" song in Figure 3–2. Repeat the song moving the starting pitch up by a half-step each time it is repeated.

11. A helpful little song about posture is "Sit Up Straighter," sung to the tune of "Are You Sleeping?"

Figure 3–2

Sit up straighter, sit up straighter
Never slump, never slump
Or you'll be a camel; Yes, you'll be a camel
With a hump, with a hump.[3]

12. Another helpful tune about posture is Jane Marshall's "Posture Ready Round." It is found in *Songs to Learn By* published by Carl Fischer, Incorporated, New York.

13. Good singing posture is vitalized, buoyant posture from head to toe. To illustrate this, draw a happy face on a small round fishing bobber and a sad face on a small light colored rock. Explain to children that good posture should make you feel as if you could float. Have a student place each item in a clear glass of water. Of course, the rock will sink while the bobber floats. Hang the bobber with some fishing line from the ceiling in front of the room. Whenever you notice posture becoming tense and unvitalized, point to the bobber.

---

[3] Phyllis Gelineau, *Songs in Action.* New York: McGraw-Hill Book Co., 1974, p. 144.

14. When youngsters stand for a long period of time, they tend to lock their knees creating a great deal of tension. Remind students to keep their knees flexible by showing them the buoyant action of a coiled spring. Springs about four inches long can be purchased at a hardware store for under a dollar.

15. A simple exercise to promote good posture involves having children raise their arms above their heads. Slowly bring arms to the sides. This will quite naturally result in a good standing singing posture.

PROPER BREATHING FOR SINGING

As children begin to demonstrate good singing posture, introduce some very basic information and activities about proper breathing for singing. Explain to children that posture and breath support are interdependent components of good singing. That is to say, good posture is essential for proper breath support, while good breath support helps to vitalize posture and the singing tone.

Breathing for singing differs from normal breathing in several ways. First, normal breathing occurs involuntarily while breathing for singing becomes a voluntary function controlled by the mind. As we sing, we can, with certain physical limitations, decide when to breathe or when not to. During singing we take fewer breaths than normal. Yet the breaths we take are deeper and exhaled over a longer period of time.

Teaching Deep Breathing

Breathing for singing is deep breathing. This involves the sensation of taking air into the lowest part of the lungs first. As this occurs, the area around the lower rib cage should expand while the chest is held high and the shoulders remain stationary. As the air is expelled from the lungs it passes through the windpipe and causes the vocal cords to vibrate. This vibration produces the singing tone. Activities to help teach deep breathing might include:

1. Help children become aware of the natural breathing process by asking them to place one hand just below the breast bone. Ask them to describe what they feel in this area as they inhale and exhale. Most

children will be able to explain that the area expands as they inhale and flattens as they exhale.

2. Explain to children that breathing for singing is identical to this process except that the breath needs to be fuller in order to support a long musical phrase. Demonstrate deep breathing for singing by standing sideways with your hands on the area just below the rib cage. Inhale deeply showing children how this area expands as the air is taken in. Ask children to do the exercise slowly with you several times.

3. Some children will want to lift their shoulders as they inhale. This is incorrect and is usually referred to as "shallow breathing." To avoid this, ask them to clasp their hands behind their backs. At the same time ask them to arch the roof of their mouth as they inhale. They should feel a "cold air" breath pass through the back of the throat filling the lowest part of the lungs first.

4. If students have trouble coordinating their breathing, ask them to try this activity as a homework assignment. Lie on the floor placing a book, stuffed animal, or beach ball on the area just below the breast bone. As the object rises through inhalation, ask them to think about what is happening and how it feels. Once this is established, ask them to stand and to try to create the same sensation when they breathe.

5. Have children work together in class to develop deep breathing. It will be important that children work with friends for this activity. As one practices deep breathing, the other observes the shoulders and rib cage to be sure the movement is correct. When they feel correct breathing is achieved, have students come to demonstrate for you.

6. Have students practice breathing through a straw. Take the air deeply down the back of the throat feeling the lower rib cage expand, exhale slowly through the straw.

7. Imagery is often useful in helping children develop good breathing habits. Here are several images that seem to work quite well:

   a. "As you inhale, pretend you are filling an invisible inner tube around your waist."
   b. "Take a breath as if you just saw a ghost."
   c. "Begin your breath as if you are about to yawn."
   d. "Stretch your lower ribs as you sing."

8. To help children feel the muscular action needed for correct breathing, have them place their hands just below the rib cage as they:

   a. Pant like a dog.
   b. Say the words "Ho! Ho! Ho!" like Santa.

Teaching Controlled Breathing

Breathing for singing not only involves deep breathing but also learning to control the amount of air to be expended for a given phrase. Children should learn to think of measuring the amount of air needed according to the length of the musical phrase. Short phrases require less air than long phrases. As children learn to measure the amount of air needed by the length of the phrase, the breath will flow more easily.

Before a piece of music is taught, it is the choral teacher's job to review the music and decide where breaths will be taken. This is usually at commas, periods, and between phrases. It is important to remember that youngsters cannot always sing the extended phrases a trained adult might handle with ease. In cases where the phrase is too long to be sung on one breath, encourage children to take quick "catch breaths." Of course, these breaths will need to be staggered so that everyone is not taking a breath at the same time. Suggest that students decide where they will breathe, citing several possibilities. This will give a consistent flow to the music while giving students a chance to catch a needed breath.

Correct breathing for singing is silent breathing. You should not be able to hear the breath as it is taken before or between phrases. If you do hear noisy breathing, you can be sure it is the result of the shallow, unprepared intake of air. You will most likely be able to identify students who are creating the unwelcome sound by their raised shoulders.

Above all, it is important that you and your students view breathing for singing as an integral part of creating the best sound possible. Breathing should never be haphazard or unprepared. On the contrary, breathing should be planned and rehearsed just as carefully as the tones that are sung.

Activities for teaching basic breath control might include:

1. Keep these words posted in front of your rehearsal area:

THINK—BREATHE—SING[4]

Remind young singers that thinking the tone and preparing the breath should always occur before you begin to sing.

2. When you rehearse the first phrase of a song, rehearse the first breath as an essential part of the phrase. Repeat the initial breath and

---

[4] Yarrington, op. cit., p. 14.

and first tone to be sure it is coordinated and smooth. Stress the importance of the first breath by telling children "the breath is the first note of the song."

3. If a phrase begins with a vowel, prepare the mouth for the vowel as you breathe. If the first word begins with a consonant, still inhale with the mouth in position for the first vowel. Consonants are sounded quickly and will interrupt the flow of air briefly before the mouth returns to the appropriate vowel position.

4. Once most students have experienced and are able to demonstrate deep breathing, ask them to inhale and exhale slowly as if they are breathing through a straw.

5. Have children stand and sing the alphabet on one pitch at a rapid tempo. Using the metronome adds fun to this activity. Start with a setting of $\quarternote = 208$. Continue the exercise, slowing the tempo down each time. As students are unable to complete the alphabet they should sit down, leaving the "windiest" choristers standing. (It is important that this exercise not be allowed to create tension in the throat or chest. Children who sing with a tight or pinched tone must be seated.)

6. Challenge students to sing familiar short rounds on one breath. This can be done comfortably if a lively tempo is used. Rounds that work nicely include: "The Canoe Round," "Hey! Ho! Nobody Home," "Shalom, Chaverim," "Old Abram Brown," "The Kookaburra," and "Scotland's Burning." More challenging rounds include "Three Blind Mice," "The Ghost of John," "Tallis Canon," "Music Alone Shall Live," and "Above the Plain."

7. To teach staggered breathing, ask all children to sing "ah" on a unison pitch for as long as they can. As soon as they feel that they are running out of air, ask them to take a quick breath and to come back in immediately. Students should be reminded to keep their mouths in the "ah" position as they breathe. The audience should never be able to detect the catch breath and neither should you. Tell children you will be trying to detect when they breathe. This will be difficult if they are breathing deeply and keeping the mouth in the "ah" position. Throughout this exercise the tone should never become strained and the volume should remain even.

8. During long phrases students sometimes try to push to make it through the phrase rather than take catch breaths when they should. The result will most likely be a harsh, tense sound. To avoid this, draw an analogy between singers and airplane pilots. A pilot does not wait until his plane is sputtering and the engines are cutting out before he refuels. He wants to refuel before these problems arise so he can be

sure he will have a smooth flight and safe landing. The same is true for singers. Tell children not to wait until they are out of air to take a catch breath. Remind them to refuel before they run out.

9. Urge students to be stingy with their air. Don't let all of the air be spent on the first few notes of a phrase. Singers should always hold enough air back to get them through the phrase. Tell students to "Keep a spare supply of air in your lungs at all times."[5]

While young chorus members need to become aware of how they can control and support their breath for singing, there may be those who find it difficult to do everything right. Do not be overly concerned with this. Remember, you are helping to lay a foundation that will support the many singing experiences children will have as they mature. Controlled breathing is a goal most singers work on for a lifetime. Even the famous tenor Enrico Caruso is said to have spent his whole life trying to refine this important aspect of his art.

---

[5] Stephen J. Ortlip, *The New Young Singers Workbook*, Copyright 1980 by Stephen J. Ortlip, p. 2. (Available from the Young Singers of Callanwolde, 980 Briarcliff Road, Atlanta, GA 30306.)

Chapter 4
Understanding and Teaching Diction for Singing

Because good diction is so important for good choral singing, and because it is an area often neglected in teacher preparation, it will be given considerable attention here. First, you will find a concise reference describing some basic principles of diction for singing. If you have had little vocal training yourself, the information presented here should be most helpful. If you already have a good background in diction for singing, this segment can be used as a handy reference for problems you may encounter with your choir.

The second part of this section will present over seventy suggestions for "how to" teach good diction to young singers. These suggestions are grouped according to specific concepts or problems and are designed to make teaching diction enjoyable for you and your students.

THE TEACHER'S REFERENCE TO DICTION

"Diction" is a broad term that encompasses pronunciation, enunciation, and articulation in speech and song. More specifically, pronunciation involves the proper sound of words as found in the dictionary; enunciation has to do with the proper sound and accent of vowels and syllables; and finally, articulation involves the physical movement required to shape and sound consonants. Stated most clearly, ... "it may be said that we pronounce words, enunciate vowels and syllables, and articulate consonants."[1]

---

[1] Van A. Christy, *Expressive Singing*, Third Edition, Volume I. Dubuque, IA: Wm. C. Brown Company Publishers, 1974, p. 81.

Diction in Speech and Song

Diction for singing differs from that for speech in the following ways:

1. Words are usually sustained in singing because they are directly tied to the note values of music.

2. For singing, the mouth and throat must be in more open positions to allow greater air flow and resonance.

3. For ensemble singing, there must be more careful attention to the uniform enunciation and articulation of sounds to insure blend and precision.

4. Occasionally, some sounds need to be modified to sustain a good singing tone.

5. In general, diction for singing must be more exaggerated than diction for speech if words are to be understood.

What Is Good Diction for Singing?

Good diction for singing is based on the uniform enunciation of vowels and the clear articulation of consonants. Together, these two components not only function to make words understandable, but also can directly affect the overall quality of a choral performance. The uniform shaping of vowels enhances tone quality and ensemble blend. The careful articulation of consonants can help to insure clarity, good intonation, and expressive singing. For these reasons, good diction should be a goal for every young choir.

Good diction is achieved when:

1. All words are readily understandable to listeners.

2. The articulation of words enhances the meaning and mood of the music.

3. Vowels are purely and uniformly pronounced by all chorus members.

4. Vowels are sustained as long as possible on each note.

5. Vowel sounds have resonance and a feeling of forward focus.

6. Consonants are sounded at precisely the same time by all chorus members.

7. Consonants are attacked on pitch without scooping or sliding.

8. Consonants are energetic but use a minimum of air.

The Role of Vowels and Consonants

Vowels are the primary sounds we sing. To make this important point clear, sing the first phrase of "O Come All Ye Faithful" using vowel sounds only, omitting all of the consonants. You will discover that you are able to sing the melody with little difficulty, but, of course, the words are unintelligible. Now try singing the same phrase using consonants only, omitting all of the vowels. The first thing you probably notice is that you are no longer singing. While consonants provide clarity for the text, most are not sustained long enough to actually carry the singing tone. Vowels provide the primary vehicle for singing while consonants bring meaning to what is sung. Stated most clearly:

> VOWELS make the SOUND,
> CONSONANTS make the SENSE.[2]

Vowels

When working with children, I have found it most helpful to introduce the following five vowel sounds first:

EE EH AH OH OO

These vowels should be sung and taught as "pure" vowels. This means they have one sound as opposed to the double or diphthong sounds found in vowels such as A (AY + ee) or I (AH + ee). Once children have learned these "pure" sounds, they have a point of departure for learning all other vowel and diphthong sounds.

As you read the description of these five basic vowels, experiment by shaping and singing them yourself. It is important that you are aware of their "feel" and "sound" if you are to teach them successfully to your students.

EE (as in *see, key, me*). This vowel has the brightest sound and requires the least amount of room in the mouth. To form it properly, the jaw should be relaxed with about enough room between the teeth

---

[2] Mabel Stewart Boyter, "Some Suggested Vocal Techniques for Children's Choirs," *Choristers Guild Letters* (February, 1978), p. 113.

to insert one finger. The lips should be slightly pursed away from the teeth to encourage warmness of tone. As with all vowels, the tip of the tongue should rest comfortably against the lower bottom teeth.

For maximum resonance, always encourage children to keep this vowel forward. The slight pursing of the lips will help to accomplish this. If the EE vowel becomes too bright, ask children to think a "little OO" into the vowel. This helps to bring the lips away from the teeth and to prevent the tendency to make EE a thin, piercing sound.

EH (as in *let, head, met*). As with the EE vowel, EH should be sounded with the lips slightly pursed and the tip of the tongue resting against the lower bottom teeth. However, the jaw and the mid-position of the tongue should be in a slightly lower position. Be careful not to push the jaw downward. This movement should be very subtle and should create the sensation of relaxation rather than effort.

Before you go to the next vowel, practice moving from EE to EH. Listen for and feel the difference as you move from one vowel to another.

AH (as in *father, star*). The AH vowel requires the jaw to be in its lowest position. This can be accomplished by completely relaxing the jaw; never force or push it downward. At the same time there should be a feeling of lift in the roof of the mouth. The soft palate should be arched, creating a sensation of opening in the throat.[3] Once again the tip of the tongue should be touching the back of the lower front teeth. The tongue should lie flat in the mouth.

The AH vowel is very helpful when working with young singers. It is probably the best for encouraging an open mouth and a relaxed jaw. Anyone who has worked with youngsters knows that they are usually reluctant to open their mouths as completely as they should for good singing. Careful attention to the AH vowel will help them become comfortable with this more open mouth position.

OH (as in *obey, protect*). The OH vowel can be sounded most effectively when the jaw is left in the same relaxed position as it was for AH. The soft palate remains arched and the tip of the tongue is in its usual position behind the lower front teeth. Moving from the open AH position, the lips should be gently rounded away from the teeth. There should be a feeling of roundness in the mouth and throat. Children may have a tendency to curl the tongue back on this vowel. Be sure the tongue remains in its normal position.

OO (as in *who, too, blue*). OO is the darkest sounding vowel. It is

---

[3]The soft palate is the fleshy area at the back of the roof of the mouth.

created by shaping the inside of the mouth as you would for AH or OH. There should be a round open feeling inside the mouth while the lips form a narrow, rounded opening. The lips should protrude away from the teeth, but the sensation should be relaxed and never pinched. As with the OH vowel, there may be a temptation to bring the tip of the tongue away from the lower front teeth. It should remain in its usual position.

Now that you are familiar with these basic vowels, practice singing them on any comfortable pitch, moving smoothly from one to the other. Concentrate on keeping each vowel as "pure" as possible. Listen for how the quality of sound changes as you move from the bright EE sound toward the darker OO.

Of course, there are other vowel sounds you will want to become familiar with. These are easily learned when thought of as derivatives of those already mentioned. They include:

"ih" as in hit
"a" as in hat
"au" as in saw
"uh" as in up
"oo" as in book

The "ih" vowel is shaped almost exactly like the EE vowel. To sing it correctly, prepare the mouth for the EE vowel with the tongue slightly flattened. Likewise, the "a" sound can be achieved by preparing the mouth for AH and widening the sides of the tongue and corners of the mouth slightly. Use AH as a starting point for the correct pronunciation of "au" and "uh" also. To create "au" from this position, simply move the lips to a slightly belled position. For "uh," the only difference is a very slight upward movement of the middle of the tongue. The "oo" vowel can be approached from the OO position by protruding the lips gently away from the teeth.

Diphthongs

Diphthongs consist of two consecutive vowel sounds in the same syllable. As you say the words listed below, notice how the first vowel sound blends into the second:

day	=	EH + ee
my	=	AH + ee
blow	=	OH + oo
out	=	AH + oo
joy	=	AW + ee
you	=	ee + OO

In each case the first vowel is stressed, with the exception of the ee + OO combination. As a rule, when singing diphthongs, sustain the stressed vowel and sound the weak vowel quickly. For this reason the weaker vowel of the diphthong is usually referred to as a "vanishing vowel."

Diphthongs can be particularly troublesome when they occur on a note that is sustained for several beats. To insure uniform vowel production, the choral teacher should be keenly aware of where this type of diphthong occurs. For instance, the word "night" in the first phrase of "Silent Night" has the vowel combination of AH + ee. To be sung correctly students should sustain the AH sound until an instant before the final "t." The vanishing "ee" sound should be sounded quickly between the sustained AH and the explosive "t."

Consonants

As consonants enter the stream of vowel sounds, they transform meaningless sounds into meaningful words. Like vowels, they should be performed uniformly by all chorus members. With the exception of some consonants used for special effects and legato singing, consonants should be sounded quickly. A good rule of thumb in this regard is to sing long vowels and short consonants.

Sustaining Consonants. Sustaining consonants flow with the vowel tone. These may be singing consonants that have pitch—"v," "z," "th" (as in "the"), "zh," "l," "m," "n," "ng," and "r," or sibilant consonants that lack pitch but have a sustained hissing quality— "f," "s," "th" (as in "think"), and "sh."

Singing consonants should always be sounded at exactly the same pitch as the vowel they accompany. This is especially true when consonants come at the beginning of a word or phrase. Prevent sliding or scooping in these situations by focusing attention on the short, crisp articulation of consonants. Generally, when these consonants come at the end of a word, it is desirable to sing the preceding vowel as long as possible before adding the final consonant.

The precise articulation of sibilants is very important in choral singing. Because of their sustained hissing quality, they can be very distracting if not sounded cleanly by all chorus members. The sibilant "s" can be particularly troublesome for children. When it comes between words or syllables, it may be helpful to ask children to think a "z" rather than "s." This sound should be de-emphasized. Whenever sibilants come at the end of a word or phrase, prolong the preceding vowel and sound the sibilant at the last instant.

Percussive Consonants. Percussive consonants interrupt the flow of sound most dramatically. While the voiced percussives—"b," "d," "g," "j"—have pitch, the pitch is not sustained as with the singing consonants. However, because they do have pitch, they must be sounded carefully on the pitch of the vowel they accompany.

The unvoiced percussives—"p," "t," "k," "ch"—have no pitch and must be sounded very quickly just before or after the vowel. They require energetic articulation in order to be heard but, at the same time, should use a minimum of air.

The Aspirate H. The aspirate "h" (as in "hat") is most often an initial consonant. It is a very useful consonant for helping youngsters learn to drop the jaw. Like all non-pitched consonants, "h" should be sounded quickly with a maximum of energy and a minimum of air. Do not neglect the importance of "h" in words that begin with "wh" as in whisper. For this consonant combination, shape the lips for "oo" as you blow the air out on "h." Go quickly to the vowel sound that follows. This simple technique will help children avoid scooping on words that begin with this sound.

Special Problems in Diction for Singing

The Consonant R

The consonant "r" is often a troublemaker for young choirs. Youngsters tend to form all "r's" in the back of the mouth, which can cause scooping and distortion of the vowels that follow. When "r" comes at the beginning of a word or between two vowels, this can be avoided by using the flipped "r." This is sometimes called the English "r" and is sounded by quickly flipping the tip of the tongue against the upper gum ridge. Try singing the flipped "r" in the words worry, hurry, scurry, and ring.

When "r" occurs before a pause or before a consonant, omit it. By doing so, you will actually be sustaining the preceding vowel and avoiding the "er" sound that often distorts singing tone. If a word ends with "r" and is followed by a word that begins with a vowel, sing the "r" as the first sound of the next word. For instance:

> "for always" becomes "fo-ralways"
> "more and" becomes "mo-rand"

Here is a basic rule about the use of "r" that should be very helpful to anyone working with children's choirs:

Always sing "r" before a vowel sound, but never before a consonant.

By keeping this simple rule in mind, you will be able to avoid many potential problems involving the diction and tone quality of your choir.

The Article "The"

"The" is sung "Thee" when it precedes a word beginning with a vowel; it is pronounced "thuh" when it precedes a consonant. For example:

"thee" apple	"thuh" cherry
"thee" organ	"thuh" piano
"thee" evening	"thuh" morning

Common Mispronunciations

In the list that follows, you will find several commonly mispronounced words in song and speech. Become aware of these and help your students to do the same.

heavun for heaven
opun for open
an for and
comin for coming
wile for while
wha chu for what you
fur for for
he yis for he is
I yam for I am
agin for again
becuz for because
git for get
ble shoo for bless you
liddle for little

Learning More About Diction for Singing

All of the information in this section has been presented in the simplest form possible and deals specifically with the problems of singing in English. For teachers who desire more detailed information about diction or guidelines for foreign language texts, the following sources are highly recommended:

Expressive Singing, Third Edition, Volume I by Van A. Christy. Dubuque, IA: Wm. C. Brown Company, 1974.

Pronouncing Guide to French, German, Italian, Spanish by Jones, Smith, Irwing, and Walls. NY: Carl Fischer, Inc., 1955.
The Singer's Manual of English Diction by Madeleine Marshall. NY: G. Schirmer, Inc., 1953.

HOW TO TEACH DICTION FOR SINGING

There are basically two effective ways of teaching good diction to youngsters. The first involves working from problems that arise in the music being studied. For example, if you notice students are scooping into the "wh" sound of the word "while," use this as an opportunity to discuss what scooping is and how to avoid it. In this case, you first need to make students aware of what the problem is. They cannot be expected to correct a problem they don't know exists. Next, suggest ways scooping can be eliminated.[4] Finally, provide several opportunities for children to perform the problem area with their newly gained awareness and knowledge.

Build on this type of experience in following rehearsals. Perhaps you will use a warm-up that emphasizes the "wh" sound. Maybe you will post a sign that reads "No Scooping, Please!". In this type of teaching, diction becomes more than a meaningless set of rules children must follow. Instead, concepts about good diction are drawn directly from the music and are reinforced until they become "second nature" to students.

The second effective way to teach diction is by introducing a basic concept or technique and then to emphasize it throughout a rehearsal. In this case, keep definitions and explanations to a minimum. Give children plenty of opportunity to perform what you are teaching. They will remember the sound and feel of their own voices more readily than your words.

Whichever approach you use, do not expect children to learn everything you want them to know about diction in one or two lessons. This is an ongoing process. Begin by introducing one concept or technique at a time and building on this. Be sure that what you are teaching can be directly applied to the music being studied. In this way, each rehearsal and performance becomes a means for reinforcing good diction habits.

---

[4]Shaping the lips for OO and blowing air out on an "h" will help to eliminate scooping here.

Ideas and Activities for Teaching Diction

Getting Acquainted with Vowels and Consonants

1. Many children do not know the difference between vowels and consonants. To build awareness, ask students to list vowels and consonants in two different columns on the chalkboard:

Vowels	*Consonants*
A E I O U (sometimes Y)	B J Q X Y (sometimes)
	C K R Z
	D L S
	F M T
	G N V
	H P W

2. Have children sing the following warm-ups. Ask students, "Which emphasize vowels?" "Which emphasize consonants?"

Vowel Warm-Up

A, E, I, O, U,   A, E, etc.

Consonant Warm-Up

Dig -ga dig -ga   dig.   Dig -ga

3. Ask children to identify where vowels and consonants are in their music. "Is the first sound on page one a vowel or consonant?"

4. Ask children to sing a musical phrase in two ways:
   a. Sing vowel sounds only.
   b. Sing consonants only.

---

[5]This is a preliminary activity to the introduction of the pure singing vowels: EE, EH, AH, OH, OO.

Ask "Which way provided the most singing sounds?" (Vowels.) "Did the singing sounds make sense?" (No.) "What do we need to make sense out of these sounds?" (Consonants.) Sing the phrase again using vowels and consonants. Use this activity to stress the importance of both vowels and consonants in good diction.

5. Prepare a poster or bulletin board around the saying:

VOWELS make the SOUND

CONSONANTS make the SENSE.[6]

Teaching Vowels

1. Once children understand the difference between vowels and consonants, introduce the singing vowels EE, EH, AH, OH, OO. Have children say the words "My country 'tis of thee, sweet land of liberty, of thee I sing." Next, have them sing the phrase. "What happens to the words when you sing?" (They are held out longer.) For fun, have one child time how long it takes to say the words and how long it takes to sing them. Because sung words take longer, and because they occur on vowel sounds, it is important that vowels be sounded alike by all chorus members. In singing we begin by carefully shaping the vowel sounds EE, EH, AH, OH, OO.

2. Use the following exercise to reinforce the pure singing vowels:

EE,EH, AH,OH,OO.   EE, EH, etc.

3. Using the exercise above, help children to sing a more forward sound by adding the consonant "m" or "n" before each vowel. The exercise then becomes NEE, NEH, NAH, NOH, NOO or MEE, MEH, MAH, MOH, MOO.

4. On a large poster or bulletin board, sketch the mouth positions for the pure singing vowels:

---

[6]Boyter, op. cit., p. 113.

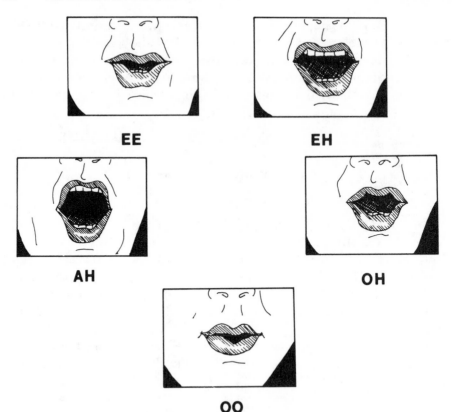

EE   **EH**

AH   **OH**

OO

Tall Vowels

Most children do not realize it takes more space in the mouth and throat to sing than it does to speak. Even after you have done several activities to encourage more space, many students will revert to speech habits. This is usually because they are embarrassed by the increased volume of their own voice or because they simply forget. Imagery and physical activities are quite helpful with this problem.

1. Ask children to sing "tall vowels," "arched vowels," or "round vowels." All of these suggest a lifting of the soft palate, creating more space in the mouth and throat.

2. From time to time ask children to check to see if there is enough room inside their mouths for an egg, a ping pong ball, or a potato. Bring one of these items to rehearsal and hold it up when you see mouths that are too closed for good singing.

3. Remind children to keep the tip of the tongue lightly touching the lower front teeth for all vowels. "Bunched up tongues cut tall vowels in two."

4. Ask children to measure the opening of their mouths by using one or two fingers placed vertically between the teeth. Most children are surprised to learn their mouths aren't as open as they think. While some choral teachers object to this method, it is very useful with youngsters who have never experienced a really open mouth position.

5. To help children feel and hear the effect of dropping the jaw to a more open position, have them place their fingertips gently at the hinge area of the jaw or just under the ears. Ask them to sing a sustained AH as they move the hinge up and down.

6. A good visual cue to encourage an open mouth and throat is for the conductor to place the tips of his fingers together in a vertical position and to pull them gently apart creating an open space between the hands:

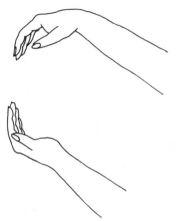

7. Clever cartoon characters can be drawn that illustrate the concept of TALL VOWELS. Hippopotamuses and alligators with their mouths wide open help to remind children to open their own mouths.

Teaching Specific Vowel Sounds

1. To emphasize a particular vowel that needs attention, refer to it as the "Vowel of the Day" or "Vowel of the Week." From bright colored construction paper, cut out large letters (12″ × 8″) spelling the vowel sounds and post them in front of the room. Around the letters write words or draw pictures of things that have the vowel sound:

EH

Ed   Elephant   Egg

2. To further emphasize the specific sound of a vowel, bring in an object that has the vowel sound in its name. (EE–key; EH–egg; AH–a jar of olives; OH–Oh Henry! candy bar; OO–a new pair of shoes.)

3. Make a bulletin board out of candy wrappers. Under each wrapper, write the prominent vowel sound in the candy's name.

EE	Reese's
EH	Peppermint Pattie
AH	Lollipops
OH	Oh Henry!
OO	Jujubes
"ih"	Snickers
"a"	5th Avenue
"au"	Almond Joy
"oo"	Tootsie Roll
"uh"	Summit

4. On the chalkboard, list a few important words from a song being studied. Ask several students to write the "singing" vowel sounds next to the words:

Free	=	EE
Bless	=	EH
White	=	AH + ee

5. Vocalize on the specific vowel you wish to emphasize. Here are two examples:

The AH Vowel

Ha, ha, ha, ha, ha.   Ha, ha, ha, ha, ha.

The OO Vowel

Coo _____   Coo _____

6. Certain vowels usually present the same problems for young singers. Listed below you will find several common vowel problems and suggestions for how to correct them:

> EE—Youngsters tend to spread this vowel horizontally, creating a harsh, piercing sound. Encourage your students to think EE vertically. Ask students to think OO, but to sing EE.
>
> AH—Children sometimes tend to make this sound too white or hollow. As with the EE vowel, this can be corrected by shaping the vowel more vertically. Arching the roof of the mouth is helpful as well as telling students to think some "aw" into the sound.
>
> OH—Be sure students don't tense the lips on this vowel. "Loose lips" will help correct this problem.
>
> E H and "ih"—Youngsters often give these vowels the same sound. Practice moving from one to the other emphasizing their difference. Repeating a series of words like "sit, set, lit, let" is helpful.

Modifying Vowels

Occasionally, in extreme ranges, it will be necessary to modify certain vowels to keep the overall tone consistent and to insure good intonation. Modification usually involves the more closed vowels on high pitches. This is because high pitches require more space in the mouth and throat. There is no specific pitch where modification should begin. This depends upon the particular sound on any given vowel.

Some choruses that are accustomed to singing well rounded vowels will need to do a minimum of vowel modification. However, if your chorus tends to have a pinched or tense sound on higher tones (usually above e^2), try the following suggestions:

1. Ask students to think "big vowels" rather than "high notes."

2. Encourage students to relax the jaw and arch the roof of the mouth.

3. EE often presents problems on high pitches. To avoid a pinched tone, ask students to arch the roof of the mouth and to relax the jaw. To keep the EE sound forward, ask students to "imagine the sound coming through a small hole in the middle of your forehead."

Uniform Vowels

Uniform vowel production should involve the same pronunciation of vowels by all chorus members and continuity of tone from one vowel to another.

1. Warm-up on the vowel sounds EE, EH, AH, OH, OO moving carefully from one vowel to another. Asking students to think a little OO into each vowel will help to keep the vowels more uniform.

2. Sing the following "Alleluia" and ask students to carefully echo:

Ask a child who has a good understanding of vowel formation to lead this exercise.

3. Rhymes make use of repeated sounds and can be valuable in teaching consistent vowel production. Ask students to think of

or make up rhymes that emphasize certain vowel sounds. Set the rhymes to music (see Figure 4–1) and use them as warm-up exercises.

Children's Rhymes Set to Music

Dan, Dan, the dir - ty old man, washed his face in a fry - ing pan.

Ed, Ed, fell out of the bed, bumped his nose and broke his head.

Figure 4–1

4. As suggested earlier, have students sing a phrase omitting all consonants.

5. For fun, put the vowel sounds of a familiar phrase on the chalkboard and ask students to identify the phrase. An example might be:

> OO, OO, ih,   OO, AH + ee, OO
> (Lou, Lou, Skip to   my   Lou.)

If children have trouble identifying the phrase, write the rhythmic pattern of the words above the vowel sounds as a clue.

6. To insure uniform vowels, remind students often to keep the tip of the tongue lightly against the lower front teeth.

Preparing Initial Vowels

When a vowel sound comes at the beginning of a word or phrase, children may tend to strike or clutch the sound. This is called a "glottal attack" and should be avoided.

1. Ask students to sing a light "h" before initial vowels to eliminate the glottal attack.

2. Since good beginnings are so important to good performance, rehearse the first word or phrase of a song many times. Remind students to "think the first breath as the first note of the song."

To insure smooth beginnings, shape the initial vowel as a deep, relaxed breath is being taken.

3. When the initial sound is a consonant, shape the vowel as the breath is taken. Quickly articulate the consonant and return to the vowel.

Teaching Diphthongs

1. Make a large poster or bulletin board listing words that contain diphthongs and how they should be pronounced:

$$
\begin{array}{lcl}
\text{Day} & = & \text{EH} + \text{ee} \\
\text{My} & = & \text{AH} + \text{ee} \\
\text{Blow} & = & \text{OH} + \text{oo} \\
\text{Out} & = & \text{AH} + \text{oo} \\
\text{Joy} & = & \text{AW} + \text{ee} \\
\text{You} & = & \text{ee} + \text{OO}
\end{array}
$$

2. Cut out large circles of colored paper from the colors listed in Figure 4–2. Write the name of the color and its diphthong on each circle. Post these in the chorus rehearsal area.

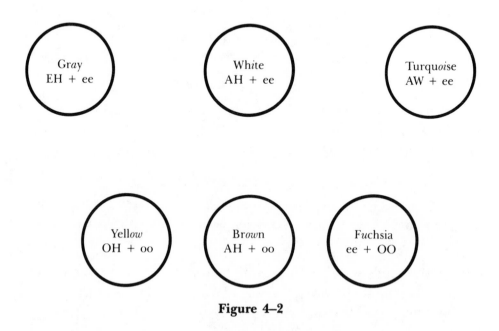

Figure 4–2

3. For the AH + ee diphthong (as in kite), Jane Marshall suggests students use "a cup of AH, a pinch of ee."[7] This idea can be applied to any diphthong that has a stressed vowel followed by a vanishing vowel.

4. If students consistently put too much stress on vanishing vowels, ask them to leave them out completely. In these instances, words like "night" become "naht" and joy becomes "jaw." *Of course, this should only be a temporary measure.* When students become accustomed to singing the correctly stressed vowels, ask them to add the vanishing vowels again.

5. Use the following examples of imagery to help students understand the stressed and unstressed vowels of a diphthong.

> Think the stressed vowel as a train and the vanishing vowel as the caboose.
> Sing the vanishing vowel no bigger than an ant or a bee.
> Think the stressed vowel as a dotted half note and the vanishing vowel as an eighth note.

NAH + eet

6. Larry K. Ball has created an excellent visual aid for teaching vowels and diphthongs called the "Vowel Flavor Chart." This is a set of colorful punch-outs in the shape of ice cream cones with different ice cream flavors representing particular vowel or diphthong sounds. It can be ordered from Choristers Guild, whose address is given in Chapter 9.

Teaching Consonants: No Scooping, Please!

Untrained children's choirs will tend to "scoop" or "slide" into some initial consonants around d² and above. This usually occurs because children have not prepared the breath and have not imagined the first pitch in their minds. Scooping most frequently occurs on the initial consonants "j," "l," "m," "n," "r," "v," "w," "wh," and "y."

---

[7]Jane Marshall, *We Sing to Learn.* New York: Carl Fischer, 1959, p. 8.

1. To build awareness of what scooping is, ask children to follow your hand gesture, moving from low to high. Start on middle c^1 and lead children in scooping up to f^1. Use whatever consonant your students are having trouble with. When students reach f^1, ask them to stop and keep that pitch in mind. Keep your hand level and ask them to sing f^1 exactly on pitch without any scooping.

2. Scooping on initial consonants can be avoided when students remember to take a breath with the mouth prepared for the vowel. The consonant is sounded so quickly, there is no time to scoop.

3. Ask children to think of the initial consonant as a target. "Aim carefully inside your mind before you sing."

4. Have children pretend to throw a dart as they "aim" for the initial consonant. "Release the dart quickly!"

5. Make a sign that reads:

Final Consonants

1. Omitting final consonants is a very common problem for young singers. This is especially true with the letters "d," "t," and "p." Bring this problem to your students' attention by speaking and singing rhymes like those listed below. Perform the rhymes in a whisper, distinctly articulating the final consonants:

> The cat sat in a hat.
> The cod was on a rod.
> The chimp was in a blimp.
> The goat rowed in a boat.

2. Point out to children that leaving off final consonants can completely change the meaning of words. Some examples are:

heat	=	he
sheet	=	she
neat	=	knee
card	=	car
boat	=	bow

3. If children put too much stress on final consonants, the result will sometimes be an added syllable following the consonant. Cat becomes ca-tah, had becomes ha-duh, and help becomes hel-pah. Even though consonants take more energy than vowels, they should never result in added syllables. When this problem arises, it is usually the fault of overemphasis by the choral teacher.

4. To remind students of crisp final consonants, use the conducting gesture of quickly touching and releasing the thumb and index finger.

All About "R"

1. To help children understand why the letter "r" is treated so differently in singing, have children sing "er" on any short melody. "Where was your tongue while you sang?" (Curled back to the roof of the mouth.) "What did it do to the sound?" (Made it "muddy," "dark.") "Now place the tip of the tongue next to the lower front teeth, and sing "uh" as in "up." "How is the sound different?" (More open, louder, clearer.) "When you sing the 'er' sound you are blocking the singing tone. For this reason, we substitute 'uh' for the 'er' sound when it occurs in a song."

2. Emphasize this same point by writing on the chalkboard a phrase or word that has the "er" sound. Respell the words substituting the "uh" for "er."

> Father, mother, sister, brother.
> Fathuh, mothuh, sistuh, brothuh.

3. This same type of problem occurs when "r" comes before a consonant as in card, word, Lord, and cord. There is a rule about "r" all choristers should know. If this simple rule is taught and applied, students should be able to spot problem "r's" and sing them correctly. The rule is:

> Always sing "r" before a vowel sound, but never before a consonant.

If you hear students singing "r" inappropriately, stop and ask, "Who remembers the rule about 'r'?"

4. Some directors feel that the complete absence of "r" before a consonant makes children's singing sound too affected. They resolve this problem by asking children not to sing the "r" but to "think" it. Others resolve the problem by telling students to omit specific "r's" knowing at least one or two children will forget and sing it anyway. This seems to provide the hint of "r" they are seeking. This is a matter of

personal taste, but *do* be sure "r" is modified so it does not interfere with good vowel production.

5. For clarity, sometimes it is helpful to have students use the flipped "r" between vowels and sometimes at the beginning of words. Children will begin to understand the flipped "r" if they are told to:

> Sing the "r" like an Englishman.
> Quickly roll the "r" (once only!).
> Get the tip of the tongue ready for "d" but sing r.

6. Practice singing words like: Amedica (America), meddy (merry), huddy (hurry), ding (ring). Of course, you do not want youngsters to actually substitute "d" for the flipped "r." This exercise is intended merely to help students feel how the tongue moves when it is flipped. After you have sung the words with "d," students will be more likely to have success adding the flipped "r."

7. Have children slowly sing a word like "merry," first using the common "r." Ask them to concentrate on what happens to the flipped "r." Some students should be able to tell you the tip of the tongue touches the roof of the mouth.

8. Sing the familiar round "Row, Row, Row Your Boat," flipping the "r's" on *r*ow and mer-*r*ily. Use this as a warm-up exercise or a reminder of the flipped "r."

Singing "S"

1. Because "s" is a sibilant, its hissing sound can sometimes destroy the beauty of a phrase. To avoid this in words like Chri*s*tma*s*, ble*ss*, and allegien*c*e, ask students to sing a very short "z" instead of "s." If the "z" is sounded very quickly, it will sound like a short "s." However, if you actually begin to hear "z," students are not sounding it quickly enough.

2. Emphasize the importance of holding the vowel as long as possible and adding the final "s" at the last instant.

3. When the "s" sound comes at the end of a phrase, be very sure to give a very precise cut-off signal.

4. Learn the song in Figure 4–3 and use it as a warm-up exercise emphasizing the precise use of final "s" sounds. It can be sung as a round also.

More Tips for Teaching Diction

1. When you are working on a new piece of music, ask children to find places where there may be diction problems. List these on a chalkboard and ask students to suggest how they should be sung.

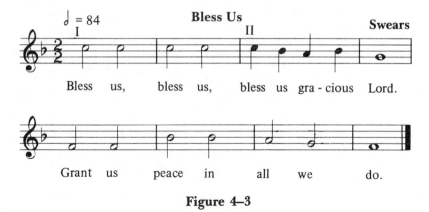

Figure 4–3

2. For soft passages, help children understand that diction must be very clear. Tell them to use "more energy and less sound." Have them whisper the words of the song. Even though they may not speak louder than a whisper, the words must be understandable.

3. Whisper in a staccato to help children understand the concept of energy with a minimum of sound.

4. Tongue twisters, rhymes, and phrases that have many repeated sounds are good for emphasizing diction. Try the ones in Figure 4–4 or write your own.

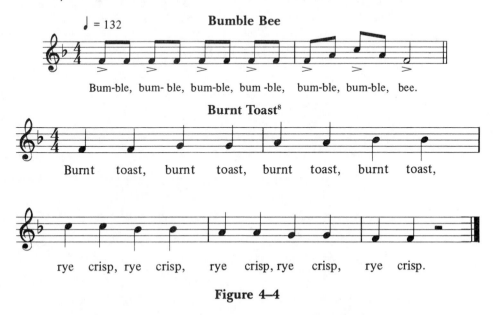

Figure 4–4

---

[8]David Held, "The Joy of Children's Choral Sound," *Choristers Guild Letters* (January 1980) p. 88.

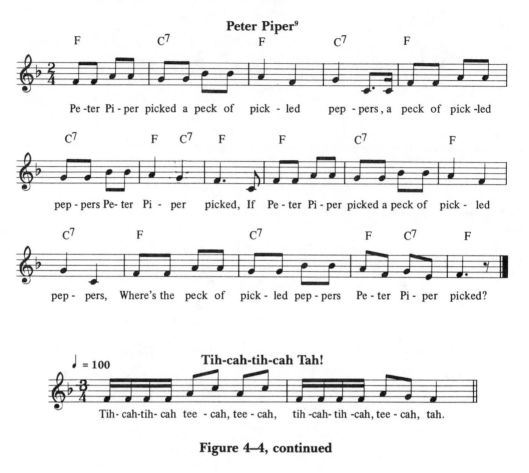

Peter Piper[9]

Pe -ter Pi - per picked a peck of pick - led   pep - pers, a peck of pick -led

pep - pers Pe- ter Pi - per   picked, If Pe - ter Pi - per picked a peck of   pick - led

pep - pers, Where's the peck of   pick - led pep - pers   Pe - ter Pi - per picked?

Tih-cah-tih-cah Tah!

♩ = 100

Tih- cah-tih- cah tee - cah, tee - cah,   tih -cah- tih -cah, tee - cah, tah.

Figure 4–4, continued

Repeat the exercise moving the starting tone up a half-step. Change the initial consonant to "n," "m," "p" or flipped "r."

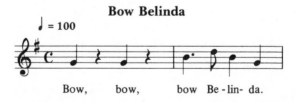

Bow Belinda

♩ = 100

Bow,   bow,   bow Be - lin- da.

Repeat this phrase moving the starting tone up a half-step.

[9]Eunice Boardman and Barbara Andress, *The Music Book VI, Teacher's Edition.* New York: Holt, Rinehart & Winston, 1981, p. 217.

5. Harriet Reeves uses a humorous approach for bringing poor diction to the attention of young singers. She suggests that students with poor diction habits may be suffering from "lazy-mouth-itis." Common symptoms of this "disease" include lips that barely move, slow tongues, and poor posture.[10]

6. Ask someone not directly involved with chorus (principal, vice-principal, speech teacher) to come to chorus to be a "diction critic." As they listen, ask them to raise their hand when they cannot understand the words. At the end of the rehearsal, ask them to rate the chorus on a four-star system:

**** Excellent Diction
*** Good Diction
** Fair Diction
* Needs Improvement.

---

[10]Harriet Reeves, *Music Today and Everyday.* West Nyack, NY: Parker Publishing Company, 1981, p. 23.

Chapter 5
Refining the Choral Sound

DEVELOPING GOOD TONE QUALITY

The children's choir has a unique sound all its own, the beauty of which cannot be reproduced by mature voices. The ideal of this sound is a free, light, and forward tone. While the tone has focus and vitality, it is never driven. There is a complete absence of tension. Tones are produced with ease and seem to create a floating sensation. The overall sound is clear and resonant.

Problems That Distort Tone

Tension

The forward head tone mentioned above must be free from tension and muscular restrictions. If you observe a child who appears to be straining (chin up, frowning, or tension in the neck), he is most likely creating some type of tension with the throat, jaw, or tongue. The result is always constriction of the singing tone. Remind these singers that "correct singing is easy singing." Young singers who exhibit signs of vocal tension are usually trying too hard. They should be encouraged to relax the jaw and to sing lightly.

Downward vocalizations on "loo" are particularly helpful in freeing this type of tense tone. Begin on d^2 and move the exercises upward by half-steps to f^2. (See Figure 5–1.) Singing "foo" on the same pitches will help to bring the tone forward.

Poor Posture and Fatigue

Poor posture can result from or help to create fatigue. In either case, tone quality will suffer. Most often, children who have poor

Figure 5–1

posture will produce a rather dull, lifeless tone. An overall lack of vitality sometimes results in breathiness or "throaty singing."

Be sure your chorus members use their best singing posture whenever they sing. An alert attitude and body posture are essential for a vitalized singing tone.

Poor Breathing Habits

Good breath support is needed to create a flexible, pure tone. While youngsters should not be expected to understand all of the intricacies of breathing for singing, they should be aware of the need for deep controlled breathing in creating a pleasant tone. Students with little ability to control their breathing usually produce a shallow, breathy tone that does not carry. They tend to lift the shoulders as they inhale and seem to gasp for air. They often fail to "connect" the breath they take to the singing tone.

If these students are taught the basics of good breathing for singing, they are able to produce a clear, forward tone that has a flexible dynamic range. Even in soft passages, they are able to keep the tone alive with a steady stream of air through the vocal bands. In louder passages, the deep prepared breath is carefully measured to insure consistent volume and tone throughout.

If the breath is taught as an essential part of the musical phrase, it will not only add clarity and focus to the tone, but also will help to insure a more uniform tone from the beginning to the end of the phrase. Youngsters who have a breathy tone must be encouraged to prepare the breath and "sing the phrase."

Lack of Focus

Lack of focus is usually related to poor breathing habits and a lack of understanding about vowel production. The resulting sound is rather hollow and seems to lack direction of tone.

Helping children to focus the tone is useless if good breathing habits are not developed. Without good breath support the tone becomes driven, not focused. So, the first step to insuring a focused tone is developing good breathing habits as suggested in Chapter 3.

The second step toward a more focused tone involves the careful shaping of vowels. Help children to feel and hear how vowel sounds are related to each other. Practice singing a sustained series of vowels moving "gently" from one to another. Children who lack focus in the voice tend to spread vowels horizontally instead of vertically. Encourage them to sing tall vowels.

Sloppy Diction

Children's choirs that have had little experience with attention to diction may tend to sound "throaty" or "shrill." There may be an unsettling shift in tone from note to note or from vowel to vowel. Pitch may be affected by a wide variety of tone colors being sounded on any given vowel. Vowels may be distorted by consonants like "r" and "ng." There will usually be a lack of cohesion in the overall sound of the group.

Attention to the uniform production of vowels is a key factor in correcting these problems. Begin by being sure all students are aware of how to shape the pure vowels correctly. Encourage children to listen carefully to themselves and to each other as they sing. Encourage children to think of the overall tone of the chorus as that of one big voice. In the end, attention to uniform vowel production is probably the single most important factor in creating a good choral tone.

Activities for Achieving Good Tone Quality

1. Ask several students to help you make a tape recording of different voice qualities. Rehearse the students on a familiar phrase so that diction and tone color are as uniform as possible. Next, record each student singing the phrase as a solo. Play these "mystery solos" for the chorus. Ask them to identify who is singing. (Students are usually very good at identifying these.) Next, ask, "How could you tell who was singing?" Students will usually give several answers such as, "I could just tell." Use this opportunity to point out that each voice is unique. This unique quality is referred to as "tone quality." The difference in tone quality occurs because every voice is physically a little bit different.

2. Draw an analogy between the differences in students' physical appearance and the tone quality of their voices. The physical mechanism that is responsible for the singing voice is just as unique from individual to individual as is hair color, eye color, height, and weight.

3. Ask several students, teachers, or friends to help you make a recording of "problem tone qualities." Be sure to demonstrate exam-

ples of nasal quality, breathiness, a pinched tone, and a dull, lifeless tone. When you play the recording for children, explain that this is what can happen to tone quality if singers are careless. Ask, "What problems do you hear?" "How can they be corrected?"

4. If children have trouble identifying why these problems occur, let them imitate the sounds themselves. Ask, "What did you have to do wrong to produce such a sound?" This type of negative approach should not be used often, but it can be effective in helping children realize how poor posture, tension, and poor breath support can affect the singing tone.

5. If the overall tone of the chorus lacks focus:
   a. Place a small red dot (about 2″ in diameter) somewhere in the front of the rehearsal area. Tell students, "This is the 'tone target.' Aim for it when you sing."
   b. In performance, pick out something in the back of the performance area to be the "tone target." (A clock, a door, or the like.)
   c. Tell children to think the tone is coming from a small hole between their eyes.
   d. Ask children to sing all tones in a "narrow steady stream flowing to the back of the room."
   e. Vocalize on the OO vowel.

6. If the tone tends to be nasal, ask children to sing as if they have a pear in their mouths. This will help to lift the soft palate and shift the resonance up and forward.

7. For a pinched or tense tone:
   a. Ask children to shake the tension out of their bodies. Start with legs, fingers, arms, heads, jaws, and finally their whole bodies. (Be sure to have a signal to get children quietly back into their seats.)
   b. To release tension from the jaw, sing the following exercise:

Yah, yah, yah, yah, yah

(Repeat, moving the starting tone up by half-steps.)
   c. Remind children to sing with their "whole bodies." Children who sing with a pinched or tense tone are usually focusing all their effort in the throat.

8. Most eleven- and twelve-year-olds enjoy discovering that the roof of the mouth has a soft and a hard palate. Help children identify the soft and hard palate by feeling with their tongues. Explain how the positions of these parts of the mouth help to shape the singing tone. It is especially important for children to sense the arch of the soft palate for creating a free, clear tone. Practice singing the vowels EE, EH, and AH, increasing the arch in the soft palate as the tone is sustained for several beats.

9. Imagery is useful in helping children create a free, clear tone. A slight arch of the soft palate will occur quite naturally when you ask students to (a) "Fill the spaces behind your eyes with sound"; (b) "Think an inner smile"; and (c) "Sing as if the tone is floating in the top of your head."

10. Warm up on a series of sustained vowels. Throughout the exercise ask children to focus on what happens to the tone as minor adjustments are made with the mouth, jaw, tongue, and lips. Ask children to close their eyes as they sing. Call out adjustments like, "Drop the jaw," and "Round your lips."

11. The ability of children to create a variety of tone colors is often reflected in their ability to respond emotionally to the words and music of a song. Ask children to sing with a tone that reflects the "feeling" of the music. The overall tone color used in the lullaby "All the Pretty Little Horses" should be quite different from the overall tone color used for a rousing patriotic song like "This Is My Country." Ask children to alternate singing phrases from contrasting selections to illustrate the difference of tone color.

BALANCE AND BLEND FOR CHILDREN'S CHOIRS

While balance and blend are usually discussed together, they represent two different aspects of choral singing. Balance refers to the appropriate proportion of sound between two or more parts while blend generally refers to the fusion of individual voices.

Achieving Good Balance

It is difficult for children or anyone singing in a chorus to hear if the singing between parts is balanced. While children can take cues and suggestions for improving balance, it is the job of the choral teacher to determine if the balance of parts is appropriate. Because the teacher is able to hear the overall sound, he or she must decide if the quantity and quality between different parts is appropriate and then make suggestions when improvement is needed. Frequently, these adjustments in balance include:

1. having sopranos lighten as they sing ascending passages,
2. having altos sing a bit lighter when chest voice is used, and
3. requiring a little more volume from students singing a melody part against an ostinato or harmony part.

These types of adjustments in balance should be rehearsed so students develop a feel for how loudly and with what timbre they should sing. In rehearsal and performance the choral teacher should use conducting gestures to achieve these adjustments.

By performance time all foreseeable problems with balance should be worked out. However, do be ready for surprises, especially with youngsters who are first-time performers. Sometimes due to anxiety, fear, or excitement children will sing as they never have before. Some of your strongest singers may become spellbound by the audience and use only half the volume they usually use. Worse yet, several rather meek singers may become inspired and surprise you with their new-found zest for singing. Of course, this can greatly alter the balance you have so carefully worked out in rehearsal. Make sure children understand your gestures for adjustment in balance and be prepared to use them in performance.

Sometimes problems of balance occur because inappropriate numbers of students or strong singers are assigned to one part. From the beginning, the choral teacher should be careful to place voices appropriately to insure balance. Keep your voice assignments flexible. Don't be afraid to shift a number of students to different parts on different numbers. Sometimes it is a good idea to actually assign several students to be "swing" singers. They will usually be your strongest, most flexible singers and are able to sing any part with ease.

Achieving Good Blend

Achieving good blend with an elementary school chorus requires: (a) well-developed listening skills, (b) uniform vowel production, and (c) a mutual concept of good tone shared by singers and the choral teacher. Unfortunately, most youngsters have no idea of what is meant by choral "blend." They are not sensitive to how individual voices must be melded to create good ensemble singing.

For this reason, some youngsters come to chorus thinking this an opportunity to show off their singing ability. They usually sing too loudly and with a forced tone. Other children are insecure about their voices and are afraid to sing loudly enough to be heard by anyone.

Here the choral teacher must not only take into consideration the sound he or she is after, but also the feelings of the students. He or she must be able to lead the overly aggressive singers to see and hear how they will better serve themselves and others by "lightening up a bit." The teacher must instill confidence in the insecure singers and encourage them to participate fully.

The ideal blend for a children's choir is achieved when the sound is: (a) focused, (b) clear, (c) uniform in tone production, and (d) free of dominance by any individual singers. If you teach listening skills and uniform vowel production with care, these qualities will occur quite naturally.

Activities for Teaching Balance and Blend

1. To achieve good choral balance, carefully assign children to parts from the beginning. In elementary school, most children can be assigned to either part since there is usually not a dramatic difference in ranges. Allow part assignments to be flexible. Often it is helpful to have a group of your strongest singers at the core of your performance grouping. If balance is a problem, one or two of these more able students should be able to switch without much difficulty.

2. Experiment to see how different seating arrangements affect the balance of your group. Some possibilities are shown in Figure 5–2.

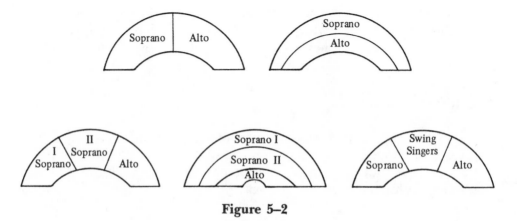

Figure 5–2

3. While balance is usually thought of as dealing with the loudness of tone, it is also affected by the quality of tone. A harsh chest tone in one part and a light head tone in another can hardly be balanced. Tone color between sections should be as similar as possible. To encourage this, have the sopranos slowly sing a descending scale beginning on e^2. Ask altos to match the color of the soprano tone at b^1. At this point sopranos will drop out and altos will try to carry the same tone color to e^1. Do this same exercise in reverse, beginning with altos on e^1. Sopranos will enter at b^1 and carry the same tone color to e^2. This type of exercise will improve both blend and balance.

4. To encourage the best blend and balance possible, ask children to sing with a full voice but "never louder than lovely."[1]

5. Whenever there is a harmony line accompanying the melody with a sustained oo, ah, oh, or hum, be sure the melody part is slightly louder than the harmony.

6. To focus on blend, ask a confident student to sing the first phrase of a song. With each new phrase ask another student to join in blending as best he can with the students already singing. Keep this exercise going until all students in one row or section are singing.

7. Ask one section to listen to the other and to comment on the blend of the section. "Does it sound like one big voice?"

8. To convey the idea of blend, ask children to think of how two substances mixed together become one. What examples can students think of? "Colors of paints," "ice cream and chocolate to make a milk shake," and the "ingredients for a cake" are typical responses from children. Build on these responses to illustrate that the end result in each case is one unified thing. "Sounding like one big voice" is an important goal for any choir.

9. When the concept of blend is first introduced to students, it is sometimes fun to play the following game. Blindfold one child who is "it" while another child selects several students to form a quartet, trio, or duet. As the ensemble sings, the blindfolded student must try to identify how many voices are singing and, if possible, who is singing. The ensemble is instructed to sing with the best blend possible to try to fool the person who is "it."

10. Use a balance scale and weights to emphasize balance in singing. Assign one side of the scale to sopranos and the other to altos. As you

---

[1]Clifford A. Holcomb, *Methods and Materials for Graded Choirs.* Nashville, TN: Broadman Press, 1948, p. 98.

or a student manipulates the scale by placing weights on either side, ask students to sing "heavier" or "lighter" depending on how their side of the scale is weighted. This type of scale is usually available among elementary school science materials.

DEVELOPING GOOD INTONATION

By the time most children reach fifth and sixth grade, they have developed the ability to sing on pitch most of the time. However, there are occasions when intonation may become a problem for the young chorus. More often than not, this will involve flatting.

Flatting may result when:

1. Children are fatigued or tired.
2. Poor posture is used.
3. There is a lack of interest in the music being sung.
4. The tessitura is too high.
5. Shallow breathing is used.
6. A series of repeated tones is sung.
7. Difficult intervals (especially those by leap upward) are sung.
8. There is a descending vocal line.
9. Children try to force chest tones into the head voice range.
10. There is a very long sustained tone.
11. Children do not know the music well and are unsure of intervals.

Singing sharp is not as common as singing slightly under pitch. However, this problem does sometimes arise when children are excited. Sharping may also occur when children try to sing music that has a very low tessitura. For this reason, music with many notes below middle c^1 should be avoided by most choirs. Both flatting and sharping occur when students do not have a well-developed sense of inner hearing. Youngsters who have been trained to "think the pitch before you sing" will be much less likely to encounter intonation problems.

Suggestions For Insuring Good Intonation

1. The best way to correct intonation problems is to avoid them from the start. For this reason, be sure you select music that lies within

the comfortable tessitura of your group. More specific information about this can be found in Chapter 8.

2. Be sure your rehearsal area is well-ventilated and not too warm. Stuffy air and warm temperatures tend to foster singing under pitch.

3. Always insist on good singing posture. An alert mind and body are both needed to insure good intonation.

4. From the start, be sure children know what you mean by the terms "flat" and "sharp." Explain that singing sharp means singing a little above the correct pitch while singing flat means singing a little under pitch. Many children will not know this unless you tell them.

5. If children attempt to sing long sustained tones on one breath, they may go flat. Encourage children to use the technique of staggered breathing as suggested in Chapter 3.

6. A series of repeated tones often invites flatting. Ask children to think of walking on "tip toe" over these notes.

7. Modifying some vowels to a more open position on high notes may help to eliminate flatting. An example of this is creating a more rounded space in the mouth and throat when EE is sung at about e^2 or above.

8. Sometimes students will tend to flat when singing slow, legato selections. Encourage vitality even in the slowest selections. Every note, no matter how long it is held, must feel as if it is spinning gently toward the next.

9. If your children tend to sing sharp when they are excited, work with them to develop careful listening habits, especially on the first selection for a performance. Ask them to sing lighter than usual, listening as carefully as they sing.

10. Working without a piano accompaniment, especially when singing in parts, is a good way to improve sensitivity to good intonation. Have children sing exercises like those shown in Figure 5–3. Ask them to listen carefully to how the parts sound together. Sing the exercises slowly using solfège or "loo."

11. If you listen carefully, you may discover the root of your intonation problems is really just one or two students. Work individually with these singers using some of the suggestions given here. Above all, ask them to sing lightly so they can hear if they are exactly on pitch. Tell these students you want them to focus on listening carefully as they sing.

12. Develop the important skill of inner hearing by using echoing exercises like the one in Figure 5–4. Ask students to "listen to the pitch,

Intonation Exercises

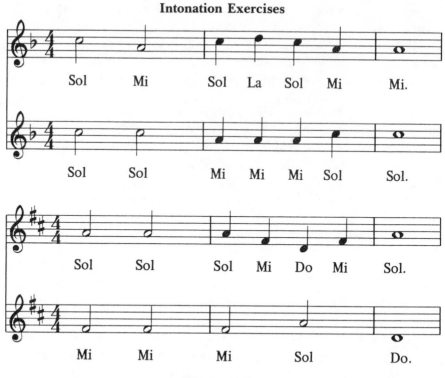

Figure 5–3

sing it inside your head, and then, on cue, sing it exactly on target."
Be sure to allow a period of silence between pitches so students have
plenty of time to think the pitch before they sing.

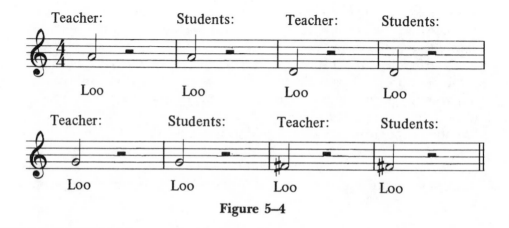

Figure 5–4

13. Ask children to think of pitches that cause intonation problems as targets. In most cases they should be encouraged to aim for the center of the pitch target. However, if children consistently sing under pitch, ask them to "aim a little higher."

14. Draw a target or use an inexpensive dart board with a musical note drawn in the center to help make this point. Place your "pitch target" in the front of the room and point to it when intonation problems occur.

15. If children tend to sing flat on descending patterns, ask them to think of the notes moving upward rather than downward.

16. During rehearsals, on troublesome descending patterns, have students move one hand upward as they sing the descending pattern.

17. If children are flatting, ask them to "sing with an inner smile." This will encourage children to lift the soft palate and bring the tone forward.

18. If youngsters tend to flat on an upward leap, have them practice "aiming for the top of the tone." Draw the following illustration on the chalkboard:

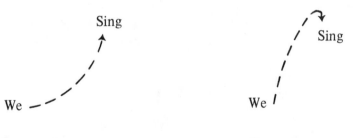

Incorrect	Correct

The approach to the upper tone should be arched like a diver who arches at the peak of his dive.

19. Sing a descending or ascending scale alternating each note between sections. For instance:

do^1	—	Part I sings
ti	—	Part II sings
la	—	Part I sings
sol	—	Part II sings
fa	—	Part I sings
mi	—	Part II sings
re	—	Part I sings
do	—	Part II sings

Check the final pitch at the keyboard to be sure students are in tune.

20. For a cappella pieces, simple transpositions of a half-step may be all that is needed to correct intonation problems. Experiment to see if a slight change in tessitura helps to improve intonation.

21. Be sure students know their music well before performance. Children will almost always have better intonation if they feel confident of all pitches and words.

TEACHING CHILDREN TO SING EXPRESSIVELY

Expressive singing is the result of the performers' empathy with the words and music of a song. At first this may seem like a sophisticated notion for children, but it is not. By the ages of eleven and twelve, children are very capable of comprehending the meaning and mood of a piece of music. They are capable of creating expressive dynamic contrasts, a variety of tone colors, and flowing musical phrases in response to the printed page and the choral teacher's suggestions and conducting.

Expressive choral singing is disciplined singing. The expressiveness of any given piece is dependent upon the attention and input of individual chorus members and the conducting of the choral teacher. No matter how disciplined a group may be, if the conductor beats out time and does little more, the music will be lifeless. Expressive singing is constantly being created through the mutual communication of the choral teacher and the chorus.

Suggestions for Teaching Expressive Singing

1. To help children understand the meaning and mood of a piece of music, have them read the words aloud as a poem.

2. Pinpoint specific phrases and ask children "What do you think the composer (or lyricist) is trying to say here?" For instance, in the opening phrase of "God Bless America," few children will know that the words "While the storm clouds gather far across the sea" were written about the time the United States was being drawn into World War I in Europe. This kind of information helps children better understand the composer's intent and often inspires more expressive singing.

3. Help children understand the meaning of a song by providing some *brief* historical information when it is appropriate.

4. Because it is difficult to sing expressively about something you do not understand, ask children if there are any phrases or words in a song they do not understand. Help to clarify the meaning of these.

5. Several rehearsals before a performance, list the songs you will be singing, in order, on the chalkboard. Ask children to suggest words or ideas that convey the overall "feeling" of the music. For instance:

> The Sounds of Christmas—smooth, flowing
> Christmas Children—hushed excitement
> Calypso Allelu—light and bouncy
> Hanukkah Holiday—changing dynamics and tempo

Practice singing the first phrase of each song asking children to think the descriptive words in their minds before they sing.

6. Lead children to understand that the different expressive qualities of each piece they sing help to make a concert more interesting for the audience. Use the analogy of a good baseball pitcher who varies his pitches to keep the hitter on his toes. The same idea is true in singing a concert. People will stay interested and enjoy the concert when there is variety in the style and interpretation of the music being sung.

7. Rehearse carefully the use of dynamic contrasts. This warm-up (see Figure 5–5) by Jo Ann Butler is particularly helpful for drawing attention to dynamics:[2]

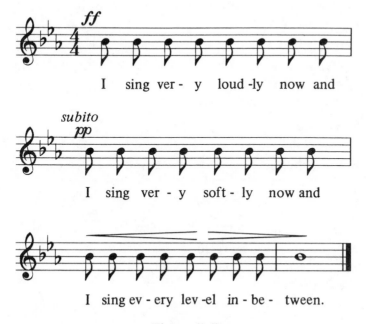

Figure 5–5

---

[2]Jo Ann Butler, "Sing-a-Lings," *Vocalises for Children* (Choristers Guild Letters, February 1980), p.110.

8. Rehearse dynamic contrasts by asking children to follow your conducting gestures. Do this on a repeated tone during warm-up or use a phrase from a song. Be sure to vary your gestures.

9. For fun, ask children to sing the loudest sound they can. At first you will probably get some yelling. This is a good time to point out the difference between loud singing and yelling. Explain to children that good singing should never be "louder than lovely."[3] For this reason, tell children you will use the terms "full singing" or "full voice" when you want a louder sound.

10. Ask children to sing as softly as they can, still maintaining a good singing tone. Use the term "hushed excitement" to help children keep vitality in soft passages.

11. Effective tempo changes require students to follow the choral teacher's cues precisely. Sing a familiar song unaccompanied. Change the tempo frequently, requiring students to watch your conducting pattern carefully. This type of exercise helps to encourage flexibility and cohesiveness between the director and the chorus. This type of cohesion is essential for expressive singing.

12. Sing the first verse of a familiar tune like "Mary Had a Little Lamb" using a different tempo, dynamic level, and type of articulation (legato, staccato, or marcato) each time you sing. For instance:

A. Mary Had a Little Lamb

   1. Tempo – ♩ = 160
   2. Dynamic level – PP
   3. Articulation – staccato (detached)

B. Mary Had a Little Lamb

   1. Tempo – ♩ = 40
   2. Dynamic level – MP
   3. Articulation – legato (smooth and connected)

C. Mary Had a Little Lamb

   1. Tempo – ♩ = 80
   2. Dynamic level – MF
   3. Articulation – marcato

---

[3]Holcomb, op. cit., p. 98.

For fun, let children suggest other combinations that will affect the expressiveness of the song. Finally, ask children to put together a tempo, dynamic level, and type of articulation that seems best suited for the song.

13. Use the metronome to build children's awareness of the effect of tempo on the expressiveness of music. Let children suggest different metronome settings for the songs being sung. If the setting suggested seems inappropriate, ask students what adjustment needs to be made. Actually let children experiment with the metronome to find the tempo they prefer.

14. Careful phrasing is a key to expressive singing. Encourage children to think phrases rather than individual notes.

15. Encourage children to "show" the expressiveness of the music with their posture and facial expression. To accomplish this, use the phrase, "Feel the music inside and show it on the outside."

16. Fifth and sixth graders enjoy learning that musical notation and symbols are part of a code for helping to remember or discovering what music should sound like. Approach learning musical symbols as parts of the "Musician's Code." Help children to understand they can learn a great deal about a piece of music by decoding these expressive symbols.

Some Expressive Symbols of the Musician's Code

PP – Very Soft
MP – Medium Soft
P   – Soft
F   – Loud
MF – Medium Loud
FF – Very Loud
　　　Gradually getting louder
　　　Gradually getting softer
　　　Quick and detached

A CAPPELLA SINGING

Learning to sing without the accompaniment of a musical instrument is an important skill for any singer to develop. The truly independent singer is capable of singing a melody or his part by himself. He is not dependent upon a musical instrument or another voice to find the appropriate pitches.

Children who constantly sing with a piano will have little opportunity to develop the skills of an independent singer. Therefore, some time during each rehearsal should be devoted to careful à cappella singing. This may include one or two warm-up exercises as well as at least one song.

In the initial stages of learning a new song, it may be necessary to use the piano for developing security of pitch. This, of course, will be greatly dependent upon your students' sight reading capabilities. Schools that have an advanced sight reading program using the Kodály approach or some other structured sight reading program may have choirs that can read some new music at sight. While this is the exception, it should be a goal of every choral teacher. Truly independent singers are reading singers. The child who has a highly developed sense of inner hearing and good reading skills need never rely on an accompaniment for pitch security.

Many fine selections for children's choirs use piano or other instrumental accompaniments. By all means, when these accompaniments enhance the vocal score, use them. However, do try to provide some à cappella singing experiences for your students. Intonation, blend, balance, and attention to individual vocal skills will all be enhanced by these experiences.

Suggestions for Teaching A Cappella Singing

1. Select at least one warm-up exercise to do unaccompanied in every rehearsal. Simple tunes like the two following are especially good for helping to develop independent singing. Teach the first exercise to

Exercise I

all singers by rote or using solfège. Sing the tune as a round. Then have some students sing measures 1 and 2 while others simultaneously sing 3 and 4. Focus students' attention on listening during these unaccompanied exercises.

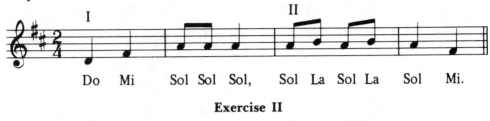

Do   Mi   Sol Sol Sol,   Sol La Sol La   Sol   Mi.

Exercise II

2. As soon as students are confident of basic intervals, rehearse without the piano.

3. Tell children that being able to sing well unaccompanied is a fine accomplishment. Comments like: (a) "You're doing so well, I'll bet you can do it without any help from the piano," (b) "Let's see if we're good enough to hold our parts without the piano," and (c) "How many people think we're good enough to sing this without the piano?" will encourage children to want to sing a cappella.

4. Select at least one phrase from each piece you are working on and rehearse it without accompaniment.

5. During rehearsal, encourage independent singing of accompanied numbers by stopping the accompaniment from time to time. Instruct singers to continue even when the accompaniment does not.

6. Use simple folk tunes or rounds for warm-up exercises. Create vocal ostinatos to be the accompaniment or encourage children to make up ostinatos. Specific suggestions for this activity can be found in Chapter 6.

Chapter 6
How to Teach Part Singing

Ideally, initial experiences with part singing should begin in the primary grades. Most often this is done with simple repeated patterns (ostinatos) being sung with familiar melodies. This approach is frequently used by Kodály and Orff music educators. As children mature, the harmonic elements of this type of approach become more complex. Through the careful selection of appropriate materials, children learn to sing harmony quite naturally. If you are fortunate enough to have students with this type of background, your job will be much easier. However, if not, it is still very possible to teach part singing successfully.

Unfortunately, some teachers try to rush children into part singing before they have had adequate readiness experiences. It should be remembered that the ability to learn to sing in harmony is much more dependent on previous tonal experience than on chronological age. Furthermore, good part singing can only occur when students have developed their ability to sing independently. This means the child should be able to sing a melody accurately and confidently without the aid of accompaniment or another singer. To encourage independent singing: (a) use a minimum of piano accompaniments, (b) work toward accuracy and beauty in unison singing, (c) encourage youngsters to sing in small groups and by themselves, (d) teach music reading skills, and (e) teach children to "sing with their ears."

TEACHING OSTINATOS AND ROUNDS

Ostinatos are usually simple repeated patterns that are sung with a familiar melody. They provide an excellent first experience in harmony for young singers. Teach children ostinatos quickly by rote. When they are sure of the pitches, tell them you will add another part. Sing the melody lightly as the children sing the ostinato. Teach children the melody. When they are sure of the ostinato and melody,

118

have them sing the song using both parts. In general, it is a good idea to sing the ostinato pattern once or twice before the melody begins. Figure 6–1 shows several songs with ostinatos that work very nicely for inexperienced singers:

Christmas Greetings

Traditional Round

Pray God bless good friends here, A mer-ry mer-ry

Christ-mas and a Hap-py New Year!

Ostinato

Pray God bless

Old Abram Brown

Benjamin Britten

Old A-bram Brown is dead and gone, we'll nev-er see him more. He

used to wear an old gray coat all but-toned down be-fore.

Text by Walter de la Mare from "Tom Tiddler's Ground." Music by Benjamin Britten.
© Copyright 1936 by Boosey & Co. Ltd.; Renewed 1963. Reprinted by permission of Boosey & Hawkes, Inc.

Ostinato

Old Abe Brown

Figure 6–1

Used by permission of the National Board of the YWCA of the U.S.A.

Ostinato

Gold and green

Ostinato

A   hu -ya, hu- ya,   hu -ya- ya.

As you can see, because of their harmonic structure, rounds are especially suited to ostinato accompaniments. In fact, teaching one or two measures of a round as an ostinato is an excellent way to introduce harmony. Here is an example of this approach using the "Canoe Song":

1. Sing the phrase "Dip, dip, and swing" lightly. Ask students to join you as soon as they "catch the tune."

2. Stop and tell students you would like them to sing the phrase, repeating it six times.

3. As students begin the third repetition of the phrase, begin singing the melody.

4. Once students have had an opportunity to hear the melody, divide them into four sections assigning each section a number and a phrase.

5. Teach each section its phrase quickly.

6. Next, tell students you will call out a number. Without missing a beat, the phrases should be sung in order. Begin with 1, 2, 3, 4 to help children understand how the song fits together.

7. On another day, for fun, sing the phrases in a jumbled order.

8. Have different sections sing their portion of the song as an ostinato while the rest of the chorus sings the melody.

9. Sing the entire song as a round.

10. Sing the song as a round with small groups providing ostinatos. (See Figure 6–2.)

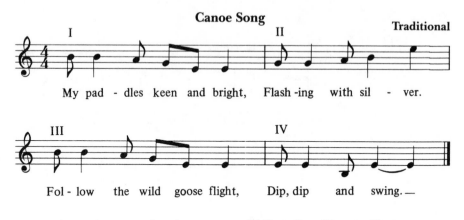

Canoe Song

Traditional

My pad - dles keen and bright, Flash -ing with sil - ver.

Fol - low the wild goose flight, Dip, dip and swing. —

2. Dip, dip and swing her back,   Swift as the wild goose flies,
   Flashing like silver.   Dip, dip and swing.

Ostinato

Dip, dip and swing —

Figure 6–2

Because ostinatos and rounds provide such a successful means for teaching first part singing experiences, several more are included in Figure 6–3. Once your students have learned these, use them from time to time as part of your warm-up exercises.

Rise Up, O Flame

Praetorius

Rise up, O flame ___ by ___ thy light glow - ing.

Show to us beau - ty ___ vi ___ sion and joy

Ostinato

Rise, O flame.

Hey, Ho! Nobody Home

Briskly   Traditional English Round

Hey, ho! No-bod-y home, Meat nor drink nor mon-ey have I none,

Still I will be mer-ry, ve-ry mer-ry, Hey, ho! No-bod-y home.

Ostinato

Hey, ho! Hey.

Shalom Chaverim

Israeli Round

Sha-lom, good friends, sha-lom good friends, sha-lom, sha-lom!

'Till once more we meet, 'till once more we meet, sha-lom, sha-lom.

Figure 6–3

Before you begin having children sing rounds in parts, be sure they can sing the melody without the piano or help from you. Be sure children are divided into groups with about an equal number of good, independent singers.

When children begin to sing the round, remind them to sing lightly and to be sure to "feel the steady beat." Some children may be tempted to cover their ears so they cannot hear the other part. Don't let this habit get started. Remind children that good part singing means being able to sing your part while hearing another. This is a skill all good singers must learn.

Most often children are exposed to singing rounds in the third and fourth grade. However, this type of part singing is difficult for some children and they may not develop the ability to sing rounds accurately until fifth and sixth grade.

More Rounds to Sing and Where to Find Them

Good Night to You All—MM IV[1]
Everybody Loves Saturday Night—MM IV, SBM V, SBM VI, TMB VI
The Singing School—MM V
A Christmas Greeting—MM V
Let Us Sing Together—MM VI
Music Alone Shall Live—MM VI, ND IV, TMB V
Come and Sing—MM VI
Poor Tom or Ghost of Tom—ND VI, SMB IV, TMB VI
French Cathedrals—ND IV, ND V, TMB IV, TMB VI
Scotland's Burning—ND IV
Toembaii—ND IV, SBM V, TMB V
Hallelujah or Alleluia, Amen—ND IV, SBM V, SBM VI, TMB IV
Sing and Rejoice—ND IV
For Health and Strength—ND V, SBM IV
Kookaburra—SBM IV, TMB IV
Evening—SBM IV
Christmas Is Coming—SBM V, TMB IV
Make New Friends—TMB IV
Lovely Evening—TMB IV
The Little Bells of Westminster—TMB IV
The Upward Trail—TMB IV
Lullaby Round—TMB IV
Why Shouldn't My Goose—TMB IV
Cherries So Ripe—TMB IV
America, America—TMB V
Chairs to Mend—TMB V
Day Is Done—TMB V
Thanksgiving Canon—TMB V
Come, Follow Me—TMB VI
If I Sing Ahead of You—TMB VI
Allelujah—TMB VI

---

[1]The abbreviations used in this section refer to the following standard elementary music texts:

MM *The Spectrum of Music,* Mary Val Marsh, Carroll Rinehart, Edith Savage. New York: Macmillan, 1980
ND *New Dimensions in Music,* Robert A. Choate, Lee Kjelson, Richard C. Berg, Eugene W. Troth. New York: American Book Company, 1980
SBM *Music,* Elizabeth Crook, Bennett Reimer, David S. Walker. Morristown, NJ: Silver Burdett, 1981
TMB *The Music Book,* Eunice Boardman, Barbara Andress. New York: Holt, Rinehart, and Winston, 1981.

More rounds can be found in:

Rounds About Rounds
   by Jane Yolen
   Franklin Watts,
   New York, 1977
Open Thou My Lips
   by Betty Ann Ramseth
   Augsburg Publishing House
   Minneapolis, MN, 1969
Old and New Rounds and Canons
   Compiled by Harry R. Wilson
   Harold Flammer, Inc., Delaware Water Gap, PA, 1967
Sing a Round
   by Mabel Wilson
   Oxford University Press
   London, England, 1964

More Songs with Ostinatos

Zum Gali Gali—MM IV, TMB IV
Bells—MM IV
Little David—MM VI
Swing Low, Sweet Chariot—TMB IV
The Peddler—MM VI
The Caravan—TMB IV
Magic Penny—TMB V
This Old Hammer—TMB VI
Turn Ye to Me—TMB VI
Dundai—SBM IV
I Love the Mountains—SBM IV

TEACHING ECHO-TYPE SONGS

Songs that employ echoing provide another good vehicle for beginning part singing experiences. The simplest type of echo song usually consists of phrases that end in a held note. During this time the beginning of the phrase is repeated by other voices. The harmony is created while these voices enter above or below the sustained tone. When using echo songs that have sustained phrases, it is very important that the sustained tone is held for its full duration. Without this sound, the harmony does not exist.

This type of echo song can be taught easily by having students first echo the teacher. Once the tune is learned, ask half of the group to begin the song while the rest of the chorus echoes. At other times have individuals be the leaders or the "echoes" for the song.

Some songs in this category combine exact echoing with variations of the echo. This type of song is more challenging and is an appropriate step beyond songs that employ exact echoing. While the majority of the song may be taught as mentioned above, some sections will need to be taught separately. Write these segments on a chalkboard or use an overhead projector. Point out to students how the tune is altered. Assign some of your strongest singers to learn this different part. Combine the two parts only when you are sure children can sing them confidently.

Be sure children become aware of the harmonies in echo songs. Ask them to listen for the other part as they sing lightly or record the echo song as they sing and play it for them to hear. Once again, use the overhead projector or the chalkboard to point out where harmonies occur.

Songs That Use Echoing

Follow Me—TMB IV
Jingle, Jangle, Jingle—TMB IV
Somebody's Knockin' at Your Door—TMB V
Abalone—TMB V
Over My Head—TMB V
This Old Hammer—TMB VI
Ev'ry Night When the Sun Goes In—TMB VI
Lonesome Valley—SBM VI
The Ocean Waves—SBM V
Old Texas—SBM V, SBM IV
Go Tell It on the Mountain—SBM IV
Old Blue—SBM IV
Four Little Stars—MM IV
October Song—MM IV
It's a Lovely Day—MM IV
I'm on My Way—MM V, ND V
One of These Days—ND IV
Ain't Gonna Grieve My Lord No More—ND V
John Henry—ND V

TEACHING SONGS WITH COUNTERMELODIES

The effective use of countermelodies in beginning part singing activities requires that the added melody be rhythmically and melodically strong. Vague "oo" patterns may present no problem for experienced choristers, but young singers with little experience singing harmony will need countermelodies that have strong rhythmic and melodic character.

Begin by teaching either the melody or countermelody. Once students can sing this part unaccompanied, introduce the second part. When both parts can be sung independently without help from you or the piano, divide the chorus and sing in two parts. Sometimes it is fun to select several "brave" students who would like to try to sing the countermelody while the rest of the chorus sings the melody.

A list of songs with countermelodies that are particularly good for beginning harmonic experiences is included here.

Songs with Countermelodies

As the Sun Goes Down—MM IV, ND VI
Jingle Bells—MM IV
Christmas Lullaby—MM IV
America the Beautiful—MM IV, MM VI, TMB VI
I'm Gonna Sing—MM V
Sing Your Way Home—MM V
The Winter Now Is Over—MM V
Battle Hymn of the Republic—MM V, SBM VI
Go Tell Aunt Rhody—MM V
When the Saints Go Marching In—MM V
It's a Small World—MM V
He's Got the Whole World in His Hands—MM VI, ND VI, TMB VI
Rock-a-My-Soul—MM VI, SBM V
Amen—MM VI
Sing a Rainbow—MM VI
Come All Ye Shepherds—MM VI
Give My Regards to Broadway—ND VI
I'm Going to Sing—ND VI
Oh, Won't You Sit Down?—SBM IV
Michael Finnegan—SBM IV
Dry Bones—SBM IV
Joy to the World by Axton—SBM IV, VI
This Land Is Your Land—SBM IV
La Cucaracha—SBM V
I'm Gonna Sing Out—SBM VI
Turn, Turn, Turn—SBM VI
On My Journey—SBM VI
Sweet Potatoes—TMB V

Down in the Valley—TMB V
Oleana—TMB V
The Colorado Trail—TMB V
Two Wings—TMB V
Steal Away—TMB V
Swinging Along—TMB V
The Inch Worm—TMB V
Roll on Columbia—TMB VI

TEACHING PARTNER SONGS

Partner songs function very much like songs with counter-melodies. In this case, two melodies from two different songs are sung simultaneously. Teach partner songs as you would a song and counter-melody. Combine the two songs only when you are sure students are confident of all rhythms and pitches.

A list of partner songs is included here.

Partner Songs

Now Let Me Fly/Ezekiel Saw the Wheel
Swing Low Sweet Chariot/All Night, All Day—TMB IV
Three Blind Mice/Row, Row, Row Your Boat/Are You Sleeping?
Joshua Fit the Battle of Jericho/Go Down Moses
When The Saints Go Marching In/She'll Be Comin' Round the Mountain/Good Night, Ladies/The Crawdad Song/Mama Don't 'Low
There's Work to Be Done/No Need to Hurry—ND V
Ode to a Washerwoman (includes Oh, Dear What Can the Matter Be/Skip to My Lou/The Good Washerwoman)—TMB V
Viva l'Amour/Down the River—TMB V
One Bottle of Pop—TMB V
Old Hammer/Me and My Captain—TMB VI
Morning/Evening—ND V
The Instruments—MM V, TMB IV
Swinging Along—TMB V

Songs with Verses and Refrains That Can Function as Partners

Dobbin, Dobbin—TMB V
Tina Singu—TMB V, SBM IV, SBM V
Tzena, Tzena—TMB VI, MM VI, SBM V, SBM VI
It's a Small World—MM V, SBM V
Zum Gali Gali—SBM V

Other Sources of Partner Songs

A Nichol's Worth, Volumes 1, 2, 3, 4 by Doug Nichol. Buffalo, NY: Tometic Associates, Ltd.
Partner Songs, by Frederick Beckman. Boston: Ginn and Company
More Partner Songs, by Frederick Beckman. Boston: Ginn and Company
Honor Your Partner Songs, by Robert Perinchief. Whitewater, WI: Perry Publications, Inc.

TEACHING TWO-, THREE-, AND FOUR-PART VERTICAL HARMONY

Singing vertical harmonies is usually more difficult for children than singing rounds, descants, and partner songs. This is because the harmony parts usually do not have a strong melodic character and because they often move in parallel motion with the melody. Children may become confused, particularly when singing in thirds, and tend to sing the "other" part.

Aural and visual training are both keys to success in singing this type of harmony. Help the children to hear and "feel" vertical harmony by using some of the following suggestions.

Suggestions for Teaching Vertical Harmony

1. Teach preparatory experiences in vertical harmony by rote. This will help children develop an aural image of basic harmonies. Some first experiences might include:
   a. Divide the chorus into two sections. Teach one part of the exercise (see Figure 6–4) to each section by rote:

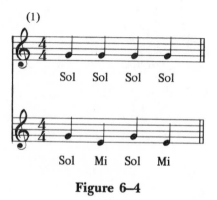

Figure 6–4

Using solfège with these exercises will be very helpful in developing ear training. Three more simple exercises are included in Figure 6–5. Notice that each example begins in unison.

(2)

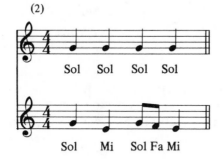

(3)

(4)

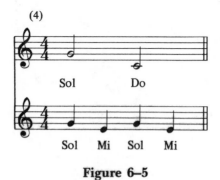

Figure 6–5

b. Build a tonic chord from the root up. Divide the chorus into three equal sections. Ask each group to "sing in" as you give them their pitch. Everyone should sustain his or her note until the final cut-off. (This will probably require catch breaths.)

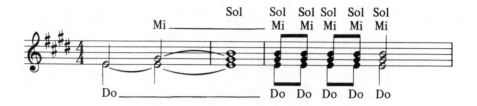

Repeat the exercise changing "do" to a new pitch. Assign groups to different notes of the chord.

c. On another day, build a tonic chord from the fifth down.

d. Use the following warm-up to help develop the ability to sing in thirds.

Repeat the exercise, moving the starting pitch up by half-steps.

e. Divide the chorus into two equal sections. Have one section begin singing a major scale in a downward direction from high "do." When they reach "la," the second group should enter on high "do" and sing the scale in a downward direction. Putting the following chart on the chalkboard may be helpful:

I	II
do	
ti	
la	do
sol	ti
fa	la
mi	sol
re	fa
do	mi
	re
	do

f. Teach children to listen for and sing chord root changes in familiar songs. Begin by using a song that has only the I and V chords as harmony. While the majority of the chorus sings the melody, invite three or four students to sing the chord roots ("do" and "sol") with you. Figure 6–6 is an example.

Skip to My Lou

Lou, Lou   skip to my Lou,   Lou, Lou,   skip to my Lou,

Lou, Lou,   skip to my Lou,   Skip to my Lou, my   dar - ling.

Chord Roots:

Do   Do   Sol   Sol   Do   Do   Sol   Do

Figure 6–6

2. As an intermediate step between rote and note reading of harmonies, use only letters to represent solfège. Put exercises like those shown below on the chalkboard or use an overhead projector. Teach each part separately, combining parts only when students can sing their notes without help from you or the piano.

(a)   s — l — s — s
      s — m — m — m

(b)   s — s — s — l
      m — r — m — m

(c)   s — s — s
      m — r — m
      d — t — d

(d)   s — l — s — s — s
      m — f — m — r — m
      d — d — d — t — d

3. As children begin to sing more difficult harmony, their ability to read, or at least follow their part, will be very important.

Before you put "part" music into the hands of children, show them how the parts are written on the page. Be sure children know how to find and follow their part. Be sure children have some notion of how melodic direction is related to printed notes. (For more specific information about preparing children to read music, refer to Chapter 7.)

4. Write two- and three-part endings to familiar songs. Put the endings on the board and rehearse them as warm-ups. Sing the song in unison, ending with the new harmony part. Some examples include those in Figure 6–7.

Figure 6–7

5. Teach children some basic "amens." Figure 6–8 shows several examples.

Figure 6–8

6. Harmonize ostinatos to familiar songs. Here are some harmonizations for rounds introduced earlier in this section:

7. Teach your students one of the "harmonies" in Figure 6–9 to accompany a recording of the Pachelbel "Canon in D." Begin by teaching each part to the entire chorus at a different

rehearsal as part of a warm-up exercise. If your students know Kodály hand signs and solfège, they will probably be able to read the melodies at sight. If not, teach the solfège and help children focus on melodic direction.

When all of the parts are learned, divide the group into four sections. (Use the recording to sustain interest.) Group I begins with melody one. As group I repeats, group II enters with part two, and so on. If you use the recording, turn it down at some point so students can hear themselves singing in four-part harmony.

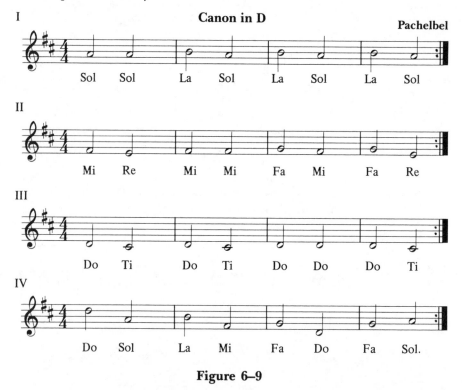

Figure 6–9

8. If your students have had limited experience singing harmony, initially avoid music that makes extended use of thirds. When thirds are used, they should be approached by contrary motion or by one part remaining stationary while the other moves to the third by step or leap:

Contrary Motion   One Part Stationary   One Part Stationary

9. Songs that are particularly good for introducing two-part harmony include:

There's a Little Wheel a Turning—MM IV
This Land Is Your Land—ND V
Ain't Gonna Grieve My Lord No More—ND V
Hand Me Down—SBM IV
Remember Me—SBM IV
Banana Boat Loaders—SBM V
Deep Blue Sea—SBM V
Winter Wonderland—SBM V
The Lord Is My Shepherd—SBM V
Gingele—SBM VI
The John B. Sails—SBM VI
La Raspa—SBM VI
Gonna Build a Mountain—SBM VI
Open the Window, Noah—SBM VI
Hahvah Nahgeelah—SBM VI
Woke Up This Morning—SBM VI
Wanderin'—TMB V
So Long—TMB V
Dust of Snow—TMB V

10. Songs that are good for introducing three-part harmony include:

When Johnny Comes Marching Home—MMV
Dona Nobis Pacem—MM VI
America the Beautiful—MM VI
Holiday Song—ND V
Kum Ba Yah—ND VI
The Baby Boy—SBM VI
O Sinner Man—SBM VI
Go Down Moses—SBM VI
The Silver Moon Is Shining—TMB V
Over My Head—TMB V

MORE SUGGESTIONS FOR TEACHING PART SINGING

1. Remember that most inexperienced young choirs will need time to work into part singing. Begin the year with plenty of good unison material, rounds, and melodies with ostinatos and countermelodies.

2. When teaching parts, tell children that each part must be as lovely as the melody. Give just as much attention to diction and phrasing in the harmony parts as you do with the melody.

3. To maintain interest when teaching harmony:
   a. Teach a short segment of a part at a time.
   b. Never make one group of children sit for a long period of time while another group is drilled.
   c. Switch back and forth between parts frequently.
   d. To focus attention, ask one group to listen to the other as they rehearse.
   e. Have children learn "the other part," too.
   f. Rehearse a short segment by rows, selecting rows at random.
   g. Use plenty of praise, especially on difficult numbers.

4. If you are able, schedule a sectional from time to time. Ask children who can come to school early to review a part. Even if a small core of eight or ten children learn something, they will help others who are unable to attend to learn more quickly.

5. Do you have parent volunteers who can take a segment of the chorus to work on parts? If the parent is unsure of himself or herself musically, prepare a rehearsal tape ahead of time and ask the parent to see that children cover everything on the tape.

6. For more difficult pieces, create several rehearsal tapes (cassettes) that can be checked out overnight or at recess by chorus members. The tapes should be labeled "Part I," "Part II," and so on. Record only one part per tape. The tapes should be clear and simple. If you have several more talented students, ask them to sing on the tapes. Tapes are also very helpful for students who have missed several rehearsals.

7. Some additional sources of good part songs for children include:

   46 Two-Part American Folk Songs
     by Denise Bacon
     Kodály Center of America, Wellesley, MA, 1973

Sunday Songbook
  by Natalie Sleeth
  Hinshaw Music, Inc., Chapel Hill, NC, 1976
Weekday Songbook
  by Natalie Sleeth
  Hinshaw Music, Inc., Chapel Hill, NC, 1977
Klassics For Kids
  by Max Lyall
  Broadman Press, Nashville, TN, 1982
Making Music
  by Robert Thygerson
  The Heritage Music Press, Dayton, OH, 1981
Simply Sung
  by Mary Goetze
  Schott Music Corporation, England, 1984

PLANNING FOR SUCCESSFUL REHEARSAL AND PERFORMANCE

Our emphasis must be on the child, not the subject. Great music has no value itself; only when it penetrates the personality and has its influence there does it really live.

Ruth Krehbiel Jacobs

Chapter 7
Organizing the Successful Rehearsal

DEVELOPING REHEARSAL OBJECTIVES

Developing appropriate rehearsal objectives is an important key to successful planning and student achievement. Ideally, these objectives should contribute to the broader goals of the choral program as discussed in Chapter 1; but unlike these broad goals, rehearsal objectives should be specific and attainable within the rehearsal period.

Rehearsal objectives should take into consideration what children already know and what experiences will take them beyond this point. They should be sequential and build on one another from lesson to lesson. For instance, you would not expect children who do not know what a diphthong is to "identify and sing correctly the diphthongs found on page two of 'Velvet Shoes.'" However, you might realistically expect students who have learned about diphthongs in a previous lesson to identify and sing them correctly in a new piece of music.

Rehearsal objectives may include nonmusical as well as musical goals. One example of this can be seen in the establishment of classroom procedures at the beginning of the school year. Assigning seats, establishing expectations for behavior, and setting up attendance procedures can all be enhanced by developing objectives for students in these areas. These procedural objectives should be established early in the year and assumed for all rehearsals.

Another consideration that almost always affects the objectives of the choral rehearsal is the pressure of an upcoming performance. While performance is a wonderful motivation for children, it can often work to undermine specific learning that should be taking place. In a hurry to prepare for an upcoming concert, the choral teacher may lose sight of the goals of the choral program in an attempt to be ready for a particular performance. Careful long-range and short-range planning can help to avoid this always difficult conflict.

Writing Rehearsal Objectives

Actually writing rehearsal objectives should begin with the question "What needs to be learned or accomplished today?" As you list these items, you are building an outline from which lesson planning can naturally evolve. To clarify how this works, let's devise a hypothetical, yet very practical, set of rehearsal objectives based on the following conditions.

It is the first week of December and you have two more rehearsals before the holiday concert. Students are quite familiar with their music. However, they are still unsure of the words in "Do You Hear What I Hear?" In the last rehearsal you noticed altos were singing too loudly on the middle section of "Stars that Twinkle and Shine." Your other three numbers are performance ready. Students know the order in which they will stand on the risers but they have not rehearsed on them yet. With these needs in mind, the objectives for your next lesson might look like this:

- To secure the words to the final verse of "Do You Hear What I Hear."
- To achieve balance in the second section of "Stars That Twinkle and Shine."
- To discuss and rehearse riser order and deportment.
- To review "Hanukkah," "Silver Bells," and "The Sounds of Christmas" at performance level.

Research indicates that teachers usually teach best and students learn best when objectives are clearly stated by the teacher and made known to students. For this reason, it is a good idea to include rehearsal objectives in your lesson plan and to write them somewhere where students can see them throughout the rehearsal.

Writing a Lesson Plan

One effective way of organizing a lesson plan is to list your objectives on a mimeographed rehearsal form as shown in Figure 7–1. Beneath each objective, answer the question, "How can this best be accomplished?" These activities will form the content of your lesson.

PINEWOOD CHORUS REHEARSAL
December 4th

WARM-UP: 1. OH _____
Repeat moving downward by half-steps to g¹

2. Practice clean attacks on phrases of the last verse of "Do You Hear What I Hear."

PRELIMINARIES: 1. Take attendance.

2. Introduce Mrs. Smith, parent helper.

3. Pass out notices for the Caroling Party.

OBJECTIVE: *To secure words to the last verse of "Do You Hear What I Hear."*

1. Put key words (shepherd boy, King, know, a child) on the board and sing the last verse four times, allowing a child to erase one key word or set of words each time until all are erased.

2. Review entire song.

OBJECTIVE: *To achieve balance in the second section of "Stars That Twinkle and Shine."*

1. Review the terms "melody" and "ostinato." Ask, "Which part should usually be emphasized?" (melody) "Who sings the melody?" (soprano) "Who sings the ostinato?" (alto).

2. Have sopranos sing the melody *mezzo piano.*

3. Have altos sing the ostinato *piano.*

4. Sing with parts combined.

OBJECTIVE: *To discuss and practice riser order and deportment.*

1. Draw the stage entrance procedure on the board.

2. Demonstrate entrance posture and attention.

3. Display and discuss the posters reading "No Primping" and "Eyes on the Director."

4. Practice mounting and dismounting the risers.

OBJECTIVE: *To review "Hanukkah," "Silver Bells," and "The Sounds of Christmas" at performance level.*

1. Stress attention to detail.

2. Strive for contrast between numbers.

Figure 7–1

When using a prepared format such as this, be sure to allow space for warm-ups and other chorus business. However, it is a good idea to write your objectives first. By doing so, you may be able to think of creative ways of using the warm-up, attendance, announcements, or dismissal to teach something in your objectives. For instance, in the lesson illustrated here, the problem of memorization in "Do You Hear What I Hear" is given attention in the warm-up.

The most difficult part of effective planning is probably creating or selecting appropriate activities for your chorus. Activities should be chosen carefully and should take into consideration the emotional as well as musical needs of your students. While each chorus is unique, it is likely that most young choruses will do best when activities are varied and drill work is kept to a minimum. For this reason, it is best to have two or three short activities for each objective.

If you find children have reached your objective after only one activity go on to your next. Every experienced teacher knows things don't always go as planned. Problems may arise in a lesson that you did not anticipate. Students may be tired or restless or excited about working on something you did not plan for. Built-in flexibility is important in these situations.

The prominent music educator Alice Beer uses the phrase "just in case" to refer to additional activities or alternative plans that may be needed at these times. What can you accomplish or work on "just in case" students are very tired or restless on a day you have planned a particularly challenging lesson? What will you do "just in case" students whiz through everything you've planned for a forty-five minute rehearsal in just fifteen minutes? The teacher who plans carefully will always have alternate plans or activities in mind for situations such as these.

If possible, it is best to evaluate your lesson and plan for your next rehearsal immediately following a rehearsal. Most likely this will not be possible. Therefore, it is a good idea to check off activities completed and objectives attained during the rehearsal. If something needs more work or if a new problem arises, make a note of it on your lesson plan. When you begin to prepare for your next rehearsal, these notes will be invaluable reminders of what needs to be accomplished.

REHEARSAL TECHNIQUES

Warming Up

Warming up should take only a few minutes at the beginning of the rehearsal. Begin promptly with a familiar vocalise, song, or echo activity. Be sure children know ahead of time that the first note or chord of the warm-up is the signal for chorus to begin. Talking should cease as good posture and singing begin. It is usually best when the tempo of the first warm-up activity is lively.

Much can be done in the warm-up period to enhance the rest of the rehearsal. Besides preparing the mind and body to sing, specific problems can be dealt with. In fact, it is a good idea to select or create warm-ups that deal with problems you anticipate in rehearsal. This might include problems with diction, pitch, tone color, phrasing, flexibility, range, dynamics, blend, or even learning notes or words.

Always try to create or select warm-ups that will help achieve your instructional objectives. In Chapters 3, 4, and 5 are many suggestions that can be used for warming up. Once you have determined objectives for your lesson, go to these chapters to find warm-up activities that relate to your needs.

Good warm-ups should help children focus on listening and creating a good vocal sound. For this reason, it is usually best to do warm-ups without accompaniment. Both students and teacher are more likely to be attentive to the singing task when accompaniment is not used.

Introducing a New Song

Introducing a new song to children is quite different from introducing something new to teens or adults. First of all, most children are unable to read melodic notation and some have difficulty reading words. The ability level for both of these skills may vary greatly among your students. Second, children often need more motivation to begin a new piece. They like to sing what they already know. They realize learning something new is usually hard work and that it does not provide the same immediate gratification as performing a known piece.

Some suggestions for introducing a new song include:

1. Play or sing the song "all the way through" asking children to listen for specific things in the words or music. You might do this either before children have seen the score or when they have music to follow. If children hear the piece before they see the music, ask them to describe the melodic line, the style, or tempo. When music has been distributed, ask them to see if their observations were correct.

2. If you have a good recording of a new piece, it is often helpful to let children hear what it should sound like when it is performed. Several major publishing companies provide recordings of some of their works. These are usually of good quality and can be very helpful in motivating students to learn a new piece.

3. Occasionally, use an overhead projector as you introduce a new piece. Ask children to follow the score as it is performed by you or on a recording. Next, select and rehearse a short or repeated phrase from the piece. As they listen and follow along a second or third time, ask students to join in on the phrase.

4. Once children have heard and followed the score, you may wish to have them sing through the song as best they can. Then, go back and isolate areas that are particularly catchy or difficult. Try to determine these before rehearsal. Keep work on these sections brief and don't expect perfection in the first rehearsal.

5. Sometimes it is helpful to practice a difficult part of a new piece as an isolated vocal exercise. For instance, if you are going to do "Calypso Noel" and your students have had little experience singing in thirds, have them learn the following pattern as a warm-up exercise:

When you introduce the song for the first time, students will enjoy already being able to perform this frequently used pattern.

6. Begin a new song by first learning the coda, the refrain, or a frequently repeated phrase. Children enjoy this type of variety. They can become bored when every song is sung from the first note to the last.

7. When introducing a new song, briefly point out why it was selected. Are there new vocal challenges for students? How will the piece fit into your concert repertoire? In short, how will the piece benefit your students and their audience?

8. Finally, never begin to teach a new song until you know it thoroughly. This will allow you to teach the song confidently and to maintain eye contact with your students.

Sight Reading

Ideally, sight reading should be taught as an integral part of the general music program from kindergarten through grade six. Instruction should be consistent and sequential. Aural skills should be emphasized as children learn to read and write what they can already hear and perform. From the earliest grades, children should begin building a repertoire of rhythmic and melodic patterns they can perform from memory and, later, at sight.

Sight reading experiences in chorus should reinforce the concepts being learned in general music. If you are the general music teacher, this should not be difficult to accomplish. However, if you only see children for chorus, try to learn what sight reading experiences they have had and build on these.

With the exception of rehearsals just prior to a performance, every chorus rehearsal should include some sight reading. This might be based on a rhythmic pattern, a melodic pattern or phrase, a harmonic passage, or an isolated interval. Not every sight reading experience should introduce something new. On the contrary, help build confidence by frequently having children read patterns and intervals they can recognize and perform accurately.

From the start, take nothing for granted regarding sight reading skills. Unfortunately, most children have had very little experience with musical scores and will need plenty of assistance just to figure out how to follow along. In the most difficult situations, some children will be unaware of the relationship of melodic direction and notation on the staff. To help these students:

1. Write several familiar melodies on the board. Sing through one of the melodies on a neutral syllable, pointing to each note as you sing. Ask children to identify the name of the melody.
2. Next, have students sing with you through one of the melodies. Point out the importance of moving upward or downward and by step or leap as you try to reproduce and identify the melody.
3. Another time, write three simple melodies on the board. As you play each melody, ask children to identify which one you are playing.

Even youngsters who have had some sight reading experience may become confused when trying to follow a two- or three-part score for the first time. Therefore, be sure children understand how parts are assigned and which melodic line and set of words they are to read. Help children identify systems, parts, measures, and rehearsal letters. Using an overhead projector, let children take turns identifying these in a piece of music they are learning.

For a change of pace in rehearsals, play "Target." The idea of this game is to help children zero in on a specific place in their music by finding a word or note targeted by the teacher. For instance, the teacher might call out "Page four, second system, measure two, alto line, third beat." The first student to stand and call out the target note or word is the winner.

Of course, achieving real musical literacy involves much more than simply finding one's place in a score. Learning to accurately interpret musical notation is a complex task that is rarely accomplished in public school music classes today. Frustrated by too much to teach in too little time, many music educators find it almost impossible to teach a comprehensive program of music reading.

Sight reading is an important part of music education that should be encouraged in every phase of the elementary music program. Therefore, the elementary choral teacher should be encouraged to take teacher training in a child-centered reading approach such as Kodály or Tometics. Such training can only serve to enhance the total choral program and your ability to be a more effective choral teacher.

Memorization

As a general rule, music that is truly ready for performance should be memorized. Good memorization is not just a matter of remembering words. To perform a piece at its best, students should have all aspects of the music learned from memory. This includes dynamics and phrasing as well as words and notes. Occasionally, if you are doing a very difficult extended work, memorization may be too demanding. However, as a rule of thumb, music worth learning is music worth memorizing.

Tips for Memorization

1. Begin memorization at the first rehearsal. Select one short phrase and rehearse and memorize every aspect of the phrase, just as it will be sung in performance. This technique not only encourages memorization, but also helps keep children interested when a piece is first being learned.

2. Assign certain portions of music to be learned before the next rehearsal. Post what is to be learned on a chorus bulletin board or have a "chorus announcer" remind chorus members of their assignment on the school morning program.

3. Memorize one section or verse at a time. When one section is completely memorized, go on to the next.

4. When memory work has been assigned, ask children to sing the required work in small groups or by rows, without music, of course. Keep track of which rows or sections do the best work and let them know by your praise that you appreciate it.

5. Ask children to think the words of a song in their heads as you play the accompaniment. When you give a signal they are to sing in on the correct phrase.

6. Alternate singing phrases between teacher and students.

7. Sing a song alternating phrases between two or three sections.

8. Chant the words of a song in rhythm.

9. Children are much more likely to remember, and sing expressively, words they understand. Therefore, look for words or phrases that may be unfamiliar to children and be prepared to provide an explanation.

10. Use word charts or picture charts to teach key words. Use similar charts to remind children of the correct words, dynamics, or phrasing in particularly troublesome spots.

11. For troublesome sections, write the words on the board. Sing through the section several times, erasing a different word each time until all words are erased.

CLASSROOM MANAGEMENT

Good classroom management helps to create a healthy learning environment and nurtures positive student behavior. It provides a framework of orderly procedures and clearly defines expectations for student conduct. It is most effective when built on mutual trust and respect between students and the choral teacher. It results in a learning atmosphere that is exciting, yet ordered.

Good classroom management begins long before the first chorus rehearsal. It begins with the selection of appropriate materials, the securing of an adequate rehearsal area, and the careful planning of long-range goals and daily lessons. Attention to each of these areas can eliminate potential problems before they arise.

While there is no magic formula for insuring good classroom management, the following eleven suggestions should be helpful in most situations.

1. Select appropriate learning materials. Written vocal scores are the primary learning material of the elementary school chorus. Therefore, they should be chosen carefully, taking into consideration learning content, innate musical value, and their interest to the student.

Music should be appropriate for the age and ability level of students. If music is too easy it may cause boredom, while music that is too difficult may cause frustration. A good vocal score is a motivator in itself. When children are appropriately challenged by a piece of music, they will respond eagerly, and behavior will seldom be a problem.

2. Secure an adequate rehearsal area. The rehearsal area should be as bright and cheerful as possible. Proper ventilation is essential and good acoustics can help to make singing and teaching more enjoyable.

Of primary importance in the rehearsal area is comfortable seating for all students. Students who are expected to sit on the floor or to share seats can hardly be expected to behave or perform at their best. Chairs should be arranged so all students can see and hear the choral teacher and have enough space to sit comfortably. If necessary, assign a set-up crew to see that the rehearsal area is ready when chorus members arrive. This can help to avoid much unnecessary confusion at the beginning of the rehearsal.

3. Plan carefully for instruction. Careful planning not only affects student achievement, but student behavior as well. Children can quickly sense when a lesson has been hastily thrown together and may respond to it with boredom, lack of attention, or disruptive behavior.

A carefully prepared lesson gives direction to what is being taught and learned. A teacher with a thoughtfully prepared lesson can move more confidently through the rehearsal. He or she knows how and why he or she will teach a particular concept and students sense purpose in the work they are doing.

4. Assign seats. Assign seats and make a written seating chart early in the year. Your seating arrangement should take into consideration balance, blend, individual singing skills, student behavior, and height. Try to seat at least two boys or two girls together whenever possible. Ten-, eleven-, and twelve-year-olds usually dislike being placed between two members of the opposite sex.

If possible, arrange and assign seats as close to performance position as you can. This will help in the development of the choral sound and will make children more comfortable in performance.

5. Establish guidelines for behavior. Begin to establish guidelines for behavior early in the year. This will probably be most successful if suggestions come from students. Therefore, at the conclusion of each of the first four or five rehearsals, ask students to suggest what might help the rehearsals run more smoothly and help to avoid wasting time. By the fourth or fifth rehearsal, chorus guidelines might look like this:

Pinewood Chorus Rehearsal Guidelines

1. Enter and leave the rehearsal room quietly.
2. No talking between numbers.
3. No talking or goofing off during sectional work.
4. Always remember your chorus folder.
5. Raise your hand when you have a question.

Post these guidelines where they can be seen at all times. If a problem should arise, point to the appropriate guideline to remind students they are not following their own suggestions for behavior.

6. Assign chorus folders. Having chorus folders prepared in advance is a big asset in establishing rapport at the first rehearsal. Little time is wasted passing out music, and children take pride in receiving their folder and discovering its contents.

Folders might be purchased by students or provided by the school or a local music store. In any case, folders should be identical to each other while unique in design or color from other school folders. If children provide folders, ask them to turn them in a week before the first rehearsal. There should be no writing on the folders at this point.

Ask several students to help you prepare the folders. Assign a number to each folder and put all music and other materials to be used in it for the first rehearsal. Everything going into the folder should be numbered with the same number as the folder itself. Keep a written record of these folder assignments on your seating chart.

When students receive their folders, ask each to write his or her name next to the folder number. From this point, students should be responsible for their folders and their contents. There should be a place where students may leave their folders if they do not take them home. These can be picked up at the beginning of each rehearsal. Whatever the procedure, children should be aware that chorus folders are their responsibility and required at all rehearsals.

7. *Establish rehearsal routines.* An important key to good classroom management with a large group of students is the establishment of routines. These consistent ways of doing things help students know what to expect. Too many surprises with a large group of children can turn a rehearsal into chaos.

Develop procedures that will help children know where and what is to be done at certain times. For instance, if rehearsal is to begin at 12:45 P.M., begin promptly at 12:45 P.M., not at 12:50 P.M. This will let students know you expect them to be on time. Why? Because what you are doing is important and, if yours is like most elementary school choruses, you don't have much rehearsal time.

The choral teacher should always arrive a little early to place the day's lesson on the board. Place your music in order and expect children to do the same when they enter the rehearsal area.

Singing is an especially good way to begin the elementary rehearsal. Ten- and eleven-year-olds tend to be talkative and fun-loving and you will get their attention much more quickly if you get them singing rather than trying to talk above their natural chatter. Begin with a familiar warm-up activity.

Taking attendance can become a tedious and time consuming problem in the chorus rehearsal. For this reason, assign an attendance secretary to check attendance at each rehearsal. With assigned seats this can be done quite easily by referring to the seating chart and marking those absent in the chorus rehearsal roll book. This can be done during warm-up or anytime during the rehearsal without taking rehearsal time.

Early in the year, establish a routine for identifying where in the music you wish to rehearse. Consistently using a sequence such as (a) page, (b) system, (c) measure, (d) part, and (e) beat or word can help to save much rehearsal time.

While prompt beginnings tell students, "This is important, let's not waste time," prompt endings say, "Our rehearsal is organized. I (the teacher) value your time and know you have other subjects and activities to go to now." Therefore, end chorus rehearsals on time. It will be appreciated by students and other staff members as well.

Orderly dismissal is important with such a large group. Chorus and your ability as a teacher may be questioned if large numbers of students stampede from the rehearsal area. To avoid this, select a student to dismiss rows that have their music put away and are quiet. Dismiss only a few students at a time to avoid noise and confusion in the hall.

8. Don't talk too much. Do as little talking as possible during the rehearsal. Most children love to sing but are easily bored by listening to someone talk about singing.

If you have an important point to make, say it concisely and then use gestures as the children sing to make your point. As in any subject, children learn most effectively by doing. Therefore, the vast majority of any rehearsal should be spent singing, with short concise comments by the choral teacher when needed.

9. Keep the rehearsal tempo lively. Move quickly from one thing to another. Don't allow huge gaps of time between numbers. This will just become "talk" time or wasted time.

Avoid drilling on music or using an entire rehearsal to work on one piece or section. It is impossible to accomplish perfection in one rehearsal. Plan realistic goals for your students and use a variety of approaches to achieve them.

10. Enlist chorus helpers. Upper elementary age children are generally eager to be chorus helpers and are usually quite capable of doing a good job. Therefore, enlist as many student helpers as possible for jobs such as arranging the rehearsal area, making bulletin boards, sorting and filing music, preparing folders, taking attendance, accompanying, and making announcements. Giving students this type of responsibility is one way of letting them know you value and trust them.

11. Discipline one-to-one when necessary. No matter how skilled the teacher may be, from time to time problems may arise that need disciplinary attention. In such situations, it is usually best to avoid reprimanding a child in the large group setting. Embarrassment in front of peers may cause alienation and encourage further inappropriate behavior.

Establishing personal rapport with "problem" students is usually the best safeguard for diminishing and avoiding disruptive behavior. Arrange to talk with these students on a one-to-one basis. Let them know you are concerned that they are disrupting the opportunity for others to learn. Help them to understand their personal responsibility for their behavior and let them know you believe they are capable of managing themselves more appropriately. Avoid threats and punishment.

Above all, try to discover things these students do well and accentuate their positive traits whenever possible. Recruit them as helpers and praise them for work well done. In short, "accentuate the positive and eliminate the negative."

PLANNING SPECIAL REHEARSALS AND ACTIVITIES

Children enjoy having something special to look forward to and will work hard when motivated by a special upcoming event. Of course, this cannot always be a performance. There will be stretches of time when the hard work of learning new music becomes tiring and the next concert seems very far away. It is at these times the choral teacher is wise to plan some "points of break." This might include activities like a special theme rehearsal, a field trip, a party, or inviting a guest to a rehearsal.

Timing is very important when planning these activities. They should come at times that complement the overall chorus schedule. For instance, a special rehearsal the third week of school may serve little purpose, but a special rehearsal in early February may be just what is needed to lift spirits and motivate extra effort between performances.

A typical events calendar might look like Figure 7–2.

The First Rehearsal

This should be an exciting and very well organized rehearsal. Welcome students and *sing*. Outline goals and *sing*. Assign chorus folders and *sing*. No matter what else is accomplished, it is essential that from the very start, the main business of chorus is singing.

Your enthusiasm should be contagious and should set the tone for rehearsals and the rest of the year. Tape record students as they warm-up or sing a familiar song. Take pictures of each section. Tell students they will hear the tape and look at the pictures at the end of the year just to see how much they've improved and grown.

Anderson Chorus Events Calendar

First rehearsal	September 24
Happy Halloween rehearsal	October 30
Holiday Concert	December 14, 10:00 A.M.
Holiday Concert	December 15, 7:30 P.M.
Warwick Mall Concert	December 17, 1:30 P.M.
Caroling party	December 20, 6:30 P.M.
Happy Birthday rehearsal	February 5
Ames County Concert	March 24
Joint rehearsal with	
Towson University Chorale	April 15
Spring Concert	May 15, 7:30 P.M.
Area Choral Festival	May 30, 10:00 A.M.
End-of-the-Year picture and party	May 30, 1:30 P.M.
School Awards Assembly	June 5

Figure 7–2

Theme Rehearsals

Theme rehearsals are particularly helpful when your next performance is at least a month or so away. Integrated into the regular rehearsal, a theme such as Halloween, Thanksgiving, Valentine's Day, St. Patrick's Day, April Fools Day, or Happy Birthday can turn a rather typical rehearsal into something special. While theme rehearsals are great morale boosters, they should never take place on a whim and should be limited to once or twice a year. They should be planned intentionally and, as with any part of the choral program, for a purpose.

Using the theme "Happy Birthday," some of the following ideas might be added to the regular chorus rehearsal:

1. Birthday decorations made by students.

2. Special warm-ups like the following:

Hap - py birth - day,   hap -py,hap - py birth - day.

(Repeat, moving upward by half steps to b♭1)

3. Asking students born in certain months to demonstrate or perform particular passages.

4. Playing party games such as Pin the Note on the Staff or Musical Chairs. (For musical chairs have only six or seven students play at a time while the rest of the chorus provides the music.)

5. Have each child write his or her birth date on a slip of paper and drop it into a "Birthday Box." Between each number rehearsed, draw a slip from the box. Students with birthdays on the date drawn may select a gift from a few small, attractively wrapped packages at the front of the room.

6. At the conclusion of the rehearsal, ask chorus parents to serve birthday cake and punch.

Field Trips

Field trips should be special activities that reinforce musical learning. For this reason, preview these activities ahead of time to be sure they are worthwhile and complement your instruction. Avoid activities that are expensive or involve complicated travel arrangements. Be sure to clear these activities with your school administrator and, if necessary, to make ticket and travel arrangements well in advance.

Some particularly worthwhile field trips for the elementary school chorus might include:

1. Attending a local high school or college concert,

2. Attending a local high school or college choral rehearsal,

3. Attending an opera,

4. Attending a local production of a Broadway musical,

5. Attending a high school choral festival as observers, or

6. Having a joint rehearsal with another elementary school chorus.

A Caroling Party

If holiday caroling is acceptable in your community, this is a "fun" activity that children enjoy and most communities appreciate. Plan caroling after your holiday concerts. If your group is large, it will be important to divide into several small groups with parents helping to supervise. Ask a chorus parent to assign several different routes for the groups. This will insure more persons are able to hear the carolers. An hour of caroling on a cold winter night is about all children will care to do. Return to school or a home for refreshments.

An End-of-the-Year Picture and Party

This end-of-the-year activity might take place at your regular rehearsal time, after school, or following your final performance. If students are dressed appropriately, as they would be following a performance, begin by having them pose for a group picture. This will be added to the photos of choruses from other years and hung in the school lobby, music room, or a hallway. Refreshments might be as simple as a large sheet cake with the word "Congratulations" on it, or perhaps your chorus parents will help you plan something more elaborate.

As children enjoy refreshments, let them hear the tape from their first rehearsal. Post pictures taken earlier in the year or have a brief slide show of the various activities through the year.

If your school does not have an awards assembly, this is a good time to recognize special chorus helpers. This is also a good time to thank chorus parents and your accompanist as well.

The School Awards Assembly

If your school has an end-of-the-year Awards Assembly, try to include special recognition for chorus members. This might include certificates for all members, acknowledging membership for the year, as well as special awards for student helpers such as secretaries, set-up crew, and accompanists.

Is it possible for the chorus to lead the student body in the school song? Can they perform a special number to be included on the program? If the assembly is on or close to the last day of school, is it possible to perform a special farewell song? Performing a particularly appropriate farewell song year after year can become a meaningful tradition for chorus members and the school community.

Keeping children motivated to learn involves much more than these types of special activities. All the "fun" activities in the world cannot take the place of good solid instruction and an attitude of caring and encouragement by the choral teacher. However, the combination of consistently good instruction with several special activities through the year can work together to make chorus a most enjoyable learning experience for everyone.

Chapter 8
Concert Preparation

SELECTING APPROPRIATE MUSIC FOR
THE ELEMENTARY SCHOOL CHORUS

As you begin to select music for your chorus, be sure to ask, "Is this music worth learning? Does it have intrinsic value that will provide students with a worthwhile musical experience? Can the music be a building block to new musical learning? What are the possibilities for learning about tone color, diction, phrasing, harmony, melodic direction, or rhythm?" Too often choral teachers select music because it has a "catchy" tune or a "cute" lyric. Unfortunately, this is usually not enough to justify a piece for inclusion in the choral repertoire or on a concert program. Children will soon tire of this type of one-dimensional music and so will you. Lyrics, expressiveness, tessitura, range, melodic and harmonic elements, level of difficulty, accompaniment, and the overall suitability of the music for your particular group are aspects that should be reviewed before a piece is selected for use. Learn to evaluate and select music based on the criteria that follow and you may find some very positive and surprising changes in the quality of your choir's performance.

Lyrics

Always carefully read the lyrics of the music you are considering. You will find that good lyrics have poetic value. They say something worthwhile and say it well. As a general rule remember: "If it's not worth saying it's not worth singing."

Of course, there are exceptions to every rule. In this case, there are many fine folk songs and nonsense songs that are too much fun to pass up. An example of this is Emily Crocker's delightful SA version of "The Drunken Sailor." While the lyrics could hardly be considered great

161

poetry, the musical arrangement and value of the piece in the folk idiom are outstanding.

Currently there are several SA and SSA arrangements available about romantic love. Children are uncomfortable with this topic, especially boys. It seems absurd to have fifth- and sixth-level students singing lyrics like, "Baby I need your love." Yet, you will find similar lyrics in print. Good judgment should tell us that just because it is published does not mean it is appropriate.

Avoid lyrics that depict a particular religious ideology. This is not to say one must avoid all Christmas or Hanukkah songs at the holiday season or that sacred texts of a general nature are unacceptable. However, it is the director's responsibility to see that the sacred music selected expresses the accepted ideology of the students and community for which it is performed. Regrettably, some school systems do place restrictions on sacred music. Be aware of the regulations or expectations in your particular community.

Lyrics do not stand alone. They must fit the mood of the music. No matter how lovely the text may be, if the musical setting is inappropriate, the piece will not work for you or your group. The cohesiveness of the text and music are fundamental to the expressive qualities of the music. Does the music convey the intent of the text? Do the lyrics and music combine to create something meaningful to sing about?

Tessitura

Tessitura refers to the average range of a piece of music. While the appropriate tessitura for various groups will vary, the music for a non-select children's choir should generally lie between c^1 and d^2. With select or more mature choruses the tessitura may be expanded by one or two semi-tones upward and downward. Be careful to avoid music that will force the young developing voice into extended passages that are extremely high or low.

Range

Range refers to the highest and lowest tones in a given piece. For most non-select upper elementary choruses the limits of the range will be $b\flat$ and e^2. With select or more mature choruses the lower range can be extended by one or two semi-tones while the upper range may be extended to g². Avoid music that has very high pitches on a closed vowel sound. High f's and g's should be few and far between and sung on an open vowel.

Melody

Once you have examined the lyrics, tessitura, and range, examine the melody. Are there awkward leaps or the extended use of chromatics? Both of these features should be avoided. Does the melody make musical sense? Is it expressive?

Some of the most lovely choral music for children's voices consists of a well-conceived melodic line matched perfectly to a suitable text. Examples of this are heard in Randall Thompson's "Velvet Shoes" and Natalie Sleeth's "Feed My Lambs." Fine works such as these point up the importance of teaching unison singing in chorus. Expressive singing can best be nurtured through the unison melodic line. Do not hesitate to make unison singing an integral part of your chorus' experience.

Harmony

Selecting part songs for the elementary school chorus requires much careful consideration on the part of the director. Never assume that just because a piece is labeled SA or SSA that it is truly suitable for children's voices. Each selection of music should be based only upon the needs and abilities of the particular group it is intended for. Therefore, be sure you know the readiness level of your chorus before you begin part singing. If you are working with a new group or if you are unsure of what a particular chorus is capable of, begin by singing rounds, melodies with descants, and melodies that have echo-type harmonies.

From here move to two-part selections in which both vocal lines are melodically strong. For children with little previous singing experience, a strong melodic line will help to insure correct part singing. Students will generally have greater success if the first note of a song or section is unison and then divides into two parts. Likewise, songs that have contrary motion or dissimilar parts are usually easier to sing.

For years much of the music written for children made great use of part singing in thirds. Unfortunately, thirds are not particularly easy for youngsters to sing. Children can become confused when the melodic and harmonic line are just a third apart and move in parallel motion. It is difficult for many children to hear the difference between parts written in thirds, and if a child cannot distinguish the difference by ear it is most likely he will be unable to sing it correctly.

When selecting music that makes extensive use of thirds, try to see that there are at least several places in the music where the thirds are approached from a unison. This brief use of contrary motion can help stabilize parts and prevent drifting from one part to another.

Level of Difficulty

Awkward harmonic elements are often the primary reason a piece is found to be too difficult for a children's chorus. In some cases, however, a chorus may have no problem with the harmonic elements of a piece but may find the range too high or too low. Some groups may find it difficult to remember lengthy and varied lyrics. Others may have difficulty with music that has subtle melodic or harmonic differences in each verse. Youngsters usually find it more difficult to sing atonal and some modal music. Unprepared or awkward intervals are also often difficult for children to sing. Interestingly, children seem to have fewer problems performing complicated rhythmic patterns than they do with advanced melodic or harmonic passages. Many students seem capable of performing almost any rhythmic passage the teacher is able to teach. Likewise, foreign language texts can present few problems when the instructor is comfortable with the text and can teach it effectively.

It should be clear from this discussion that the difficulty of a piece is relative to the ability of the group for whom it is intended and the skill of the choral teacher. Therefore, very careful and subjective judgment must be used in this regard. While children love to be challenged, they will become frustrated if the music is consistently too difficult. Likewise, if the music is too easy, they will learn it quickly and become bored.

Accompaniment

The accompaniment of a piece of music should enhance the text and the overall effect of the song. From the start, the introduction should set the tone of what is to come. Therefore, look for accompaniments whose introductions make interesting and appropriate opening statements. Look for accompaniments that do not double the vocal line. Avoid accompaniments that overshadow the vocal line with grandiose chords and arpeggios. A good accompaniment will give gentle support to the vocal line. It will not overpower it. Furthermore, a good accompaniment will add variety and color to a work.

Of course, it is also important to consider the ability and talents of your accompanist. If you select a piece knowing it will be too difficult for your accompanist, you are asking for trouble. A beautifully conceived piece of music will not be beautifully performed if it is beyond the ability of the performer.

Suitability to Your Group

The final criterion for selecting appropriate music for the elementry chorus should be its overall suitability for your particular group. Try to imagine your chorus performing the piece. Will they enjoy learning and performing it? Will they feel a sense of pride and accomplishment presenting it to an audience? Does the overall character of the piece fit the needs of your group? Will you enjoy conducting it?

While it is true that every chorus will differ in ability and that careful selection of music should be based on the particular needs of your group, you will discover certain pieces that always seem worth teaching. They may teach a concept very well or be delightful additions to almost any concert program. Keep a file of all such pieces. As you review new works, add to the file those that meet your criteria. Over the years this collection will become your main resource for program building.

*Some Suggested Choral Music
for the Non-Select Children's Chorus*

In Figure 8–1, you will find thirty-one compositions particularly well written for the non-select children's chorus. With a few exceptions, this music adheres to the guidelines for selection given earlier in this chapter.

Title	Arrangement	Composer/Arranger	Publisher
A Child Was Born	Unison	Carey Blyton	G. Schirmer 11631
A Joyous Psalm	Unison	Eugene Butler	Choristers Guild A–74
A Voice from a Dream	2-Part	Joyce Elaine Eilers	Belwin Mills SCHCH 2130
A Whistling Carol	Unison	Hal H. Hopson	Choristers Guild A–258
All the Pretty Little Horses	2-Part	Ruth Artman	Studio P/R V–7932
Angels We Have Heard on High	2-Part	Margaret Shelly Vance	Belwin Mills 2021
Calypso Allelu	2-Part	Jill Gallina	Shawnee Press E–243
Cripple Creek	2-Part	Emily Crocker	Jenson 423–03032
Ding Dong! Merrily on High!	2-Part	Ruth Artman	Hal Leonard 08571800
Every Morning's Sun	Unison	Sue Ellen Page	Choristers Guild A–193
Feed My Lambs	Unison	Natalie Sleeth	Carl Fischer CM 7777
The Gift of Love	2-Part	Hal Hopson	Hope CF 148
God Bless America	2-Part	Berlin/Eilers	Jenson 402–07012
God of Great and God of Small	Unison	Natalie Sleeth	Carl Fischer CM 7808
Grace, Peace unto You	2-Part	Michael Jothen	Coronet Press CP 211
Hanukkah Holiday	2-Part	Linda Swears	Shawnee Press EA–29
Hanukkah is Here	2-Part	Linda Swears	Shawnee Press EA–39
Hosanna in the Highest	2-Part	Audrey Snyder	Studio P/R V–7931
My Father's House	2-Part	Aden Lewis	Plymouth Sc–509
Promised Land	2-Part	Natalie Sleeth	Sacred Music Press S–5775
Ring Those Christmas Bells	2-Part	Martha Sobaje	Kendor Music 4368
Send Down the Rain	2-Part	Joyce Eilers	Jenson 402–19052
Sing Me a Song of the Land I Love	2-Part	Knox and Wilson	Jenson 409–19042
Sing We a Carol Low	Unison	Eugene Butler	Carl Fischer CM 8092
Stars That Twinkle and Shine	2-Part	Joyce Eilers	Jenson 402–19042
The Drunken Sailor	2-Part	Emily Crocker	Jenson 423–04012
The Guitar Man	2-Part	Audrey Snyder	Jenson 423–07012
The Lord Is My Shepherd	2-Part	Jill Gallina	Coronet Press CP–103
The Sounds of Christmas	2-Part	Linda Swears	Shawnee Press E–224
This Is My Country	2-Part	Jacobs/Emerson	Jenson 403–20022
Velvet Shoes	2-Part	Randall Thompson	E. C. Schirmer 2526
We Want to Sing	2-Part	Roger Emerson	Jenson 403–23022

Figure 8–1

Title	Arrangement	Composer/Arranger	Publisher
A Song Is a Gift to God	3-Part	Mary Caldwell	Carl Fischer CM 7874
Adoramus Te	2-Part	Palestrina/Swift	Belwin Mills 1649
Alleluia (from Cantata #142)	2-Part	Bach/Ehret	Edward Marks MC 4311
Alleluia	2-Part	Boyce/Kirk	Pro Art Pro Ch. 2381
Americana	2-Part	Luigi Zaninelli	Shawnee Press E–120
Calypso Noel	2-Part	Krunnfusz	Shawnee Press A–884
Carol of the Shepherd Children	3-Part	Joyce Eilers	Hal Leonard 0854 1500
Come Glad Hearts	2-Part	Mozart/Kemp	Choristers Guild R–14
Come, Sing This Round with Me	2-Part	Martini/Greyson	Bourne B236 844–351
Echo	2-Part	David Smart	Somerset Press SP 699
He Is Born	3-Part	Joyce Eilers	Schmitt 2904
If Ye Would Hear the Angels Sing	2-Part	Douglas Wagner	Coronet Press CP 214
Jesu, Joy of Man's Desiring	2-Part	Bach/Mattfeld	E. C. Schirmer 2508
Little Miss Muffet	2-Part	Hal Hopson	Shawnee Press E–128
Praise Ye the Lord (From the "Christmas Oratorio")	2-Part	Saint-Saëns/Ehret	Boosey and Hawkes 5285
Roundelay Noel	2-Part	Gordon Young	Shawnee Press E–64
Serve Bone	2-Part	Orlando di Lasso	Mark Foster MF 801
Selections from "Stabat Mater"	2-Part	G. B. Pergolesi	G. Schirmer Ed. 498
The Dove and the Maple Tree	2-Part	Anton Dvořák	Walton Music WH–141
The Sleigh	2-Part	Kountz/Riegger	G. Schirmer 7635
Three Hungarian Folk Songs	2-Part	Matyas Seiber	G. Schirmer 10826
Solfeggio	2-Part	Maxwell/Wilson	Robbins R 3876
Stars Are for Those Who Lift Their Eyes	Unison or 2-Part	Pauline Delmonte	Choristers Guild A–117

Figure 8–2

Some Suggested Choral Music for the Select or Advanced Children's Chorus

The music suggested in Figure 8–2 is generally more difficult than that found in the previous list. Harmonic structure, range and tessitura, and the use of more sophisticated or foreign language texts make these selections more appropriate for advanced groups.

These choral selections represent works this author has found particularly well suited for children's choirs. However, the choral teacher should keep in mind the vast resources of folk and art song literature available. Many suitable part songs and rounds can be found in Chapter 6 and most general music series also have a suitable repertoire.

Four additional resources to help you select music for children's chorus are:

1. *Music For Children's Choirs*
   A Selective and Graded Listing
   MENC
   1902 Association Drive
   Reston, VA 22091
2. Support Services
   (exclusive distributor of Kodály Center of America publications)
   P.O. Box 478
   Natick, MA 01760
3. *The Juilliard Repertory Library*
   (songs collected by the Juilliard Repertory Project)
   Canyon Press
   P.O. Box 12135
   Cincinnati, OH 45201
4. "The Selection of Significant Choral Music for Children's Voices"
   (an article and suggested listing of music for children's choirs)
   by Doreen Rao
   Choristers Guild Newsletter, Vol. XXII, No. 6, February 1981, page 101

Of course, new music is constantly being published and can be obtained for review by writing to publishers. For this reason, a list of publishers and their addresses can be found in Chapter 9.

CONCERT THEMES AND PROGRAM BUILDING

Choosing a Concert Theme

Ideally, the selection of a concert theme and program building should be based on music appropriate for learning and performance by your group. Whenever possible, let themes and program ideas come from well selected music rather than trying to work around a predetermined theme.

However, themes must take into consideration the format of the total music program. In the elementary school, a choral concert featuring only the chorus is rare. Usually school concerts include a shared program by band, orchestra, and chorus or the chorus performs as part of an all-school program. Therefore, themes should be broad enough to cover a wide variety of musical performance and should be determined jointly by all persons having performance groups on the program.

Some possible themes for elementary school concerts and programs might include:

Winter Holiday Themes

Because It's Christmas

Christmas Around the World

Christmas Here and There

Christmas Memories

Happy Holidays

Holiday Blessings

Holiday Sounds

It's Beginning to Look a Lot Like Christmas

It's Christmas!

Sing We Now of Christmas

Songs for the Season

The Gift of Song

The Gifts We Bring

The Sounds of Christmas

A Winter Holiday

Patriotic Themes

A Salute to America

A Salute to Freedom

A Salute to the Land I Love

From Sea to Shining Sea

Let Freedom Sing

Music of America

Of Thee We Sing

Sing Out for America

Songs of Freedom

Sweet Land of Mine

We Sing of Freedom

Spring and General Themes

A Musical Potpourri

Blessed with a Song

Everything's Comin' Up Music

From Bach to Rock

Lift Every Voice and Sing

Make Mine Music

Music Now and Then

Music, Music, Music

Music, Sweet Music

Sing a Happy Song

Something to Sing About

The Gift of Song

There's Music in the Air

Program Building

Organize choral performance with two primary concerns in mind—what will provide the best performance order for the chorus and what will be the most satisfactory presentation as a whole for the audience?

The Pinewood Elementary School
Band and Chorus

present

THE SOUNDS OF CHRISTMAS

Chorus

The Sounds of Christmas......................Linda Swears
Angels We Have Heard on High....Arr. by Margaret Shelley Vance
Roundelay Noel..............Gordan Young and Joyce Merman

Orchestra

O Come, Little Children.................Arr. by Edward Jurey
Christmas Is Here......................Arr. by Edward Jurey

String Quartet

O Come All Ye Faithful........................John Reading
Arr. by Corwin Taylor

Advanced Vocal Music

Carol of the Shepherd Children...................Joyce Eilers
Alleluia.....................................William Boyce
Arr. by Theron Kirk

Band

Good King Wenceslaus....................Arr. by John Kinyon
Jingle Bells Around the World.............Arr. Andrew Balent

Chorus

Hi Ho for Hanukkah.....................Betsy Jo Angebranndt
Stars That Twinkle and Shine ....Joyce Eilers
The Sounds of Christmas (Reprise)
    *O Come All Ye Faithful
    *Silent Night
    *Joy to the World

*The audience is invited to join the chorus in singing the first
verse of each of these carols.

Figure 8–3

In general, it is best to begin with something the chorus especially enjoys and sings well. A quick tempo is a plus for an opening number since it engages the audience most readily. The first number on a program can be rather short. It should let the audience know you are eager to perform for them. Throughout the program, use a variety of pieces that differ in style, tempo, and the use of instrumental accompaniments. Longer works are best included early in the program. The final number can be a particularly exciting one or it might be something rather sentimental such as a chorus theme song or a "farewell."

The Rockford Elementary School Chorus
presents

A HOLIDAY SING-ALONG

at

Charles Center
December 15, 19—

Sing-Along

*O Come All Ye Faithful..........................Latin Hymn
*Deck the Halls...............................Old Welsh Air

Chorus

Stars Are for Those Who Lift Their Eyes ......Pauline Delmonte
Calypso Noel ....Gordon Krunnfusz
Ring Those Christmas Bells....................Martha Sobaje

Sing-Along

*O Little Town of Bethlehem ....Lewis Redner
*Angels We Have Heard on High ....Old French Melody

Chorus

Hanukkah Holiday.............................Linda Swears
He Is Born ....Joyce Eilers

Sing-Along

*Rudolph the Red-Nosed Reindeer...............Johnny Marks
*Joy to the World ....Isaac Watts, George Frederick Handel

*The words to these carols are found on the back of your program.

Figure 8–4

Vary the performance by using soloists, small groups, and talented instrumentalists. Simple choreography can be a nice addition if it does not take away from the singing.

Don't try to do too many numbers on one program. It is far better to have three or four well-prepared selections than eight or ten that are

---

SING A HAPPY SONG
presented by
The Lutherville Elementary School Chorus

Chorus

Sing a Happy Song
Linda Swears

My Father's House
Aden Lewis

God Bless America
Irving Berlin
Arr. by Joyce Eilers

Advanced Vocal Music

Three Hungarian Folk Songs
"The Handsome Butcher"
"Apple, Apple"
"The Old Woman"
A. L. Lloyd and Matyas Seiber
Shena Molyneaux, Piano Soloist
Allegro from Sonata Op. 2, No. 1
Ludwig van Beethoven

Chorus

Send Down the Rain
Joyce Eilers

*Every Morning's Sun
Sue Ellen Page

Cripple Creek
Emily Crocker

Blessed with a Song
Linda Swears

*Accompanists: Susan Robinson and Ellen Buckly

Figure 8–5

really not performance-ready. For a beginning upper elementary school chorus that meets once a week, four or five numbers, three in parts and two in unison, can usually be prepared adequately for a December concert. The spring repertoire can be considerably larger, including numbers learned between January and March and others learned in March, April, and May.

In the sample programs in Figures 8–3, 8–4 and 8–5, notice the winter programs include instrumental music and familiar carols to round out an interesting program. The spring program has the chorus performing several more numbers, but still makes use of special groups and soloists to add variety to the program.

STEP-BY-STEP PRE-CONCERT PLANNING

For many children, the chorus concert will be a first experience before an audience. Therefore, the attitude and expectations they bring to the experience need to be carefully nurtured. Thoughtful and thorough pre-concert planning should help to insure a good performance experience for children as well as their audience. Youngsters need to know what, where, when, and how they are expected to perform. If this information is not discussed and integrated into rehearsals in advance, a good deal of unnecessary confusion may result.

Performance should be a natural outgrowth of the choral learning experience. A healthy student attitude to be developed throughout chorus rehearsals might be: "We have studied and worked hard to create the most beautiful music possible. Now it is time to share our music with others."

Children do not respond favorably to last minute rush or confusion. Try to avoid throwing things together at the last minute. No matter how hard your children have worked or how beautifully they sing, haphazard pre-concert preparation may result in a performance far below your students' ability and your expectations.

Below you will find some guidelines for pre-concert planning. Of course, not all of these will be appropriate for every situation. However, as you begin to prepare for a concert, look over the list to make sure you're not forgetting any important details.

One Month Prior to Performance

1. Enlist someone to design a program cover. If posters and publicity are desired, these should be prepared and posted at this time.

2. If transportation needs to be arranged, do so at least a month in advance.

3. If children are performing away from school, go to the place several weeks before to see what the facilities and acoustics are like. Is there a piano? Is it in tune? Are there risers? Is there an adequate warm-up area?

4. Have a chorus parent organize other parents who will help to chaperone children.

Three Weeks Prior to Performance

1. If your accompanist has been unable to attend all rehearsals, be sure he or she is able to attend no less than three rehearsals prior to the performance.

2. Send permission slips home to be returned to you at least one week prior to the concert. This notice should include the exact time and place of the performance, what students are to wear and, if the concert is away from school, when students will return.

3. Throughout this period, begin to simulate actual concert decorum as much as possible. Begin to rehearse proper performance posture.

4. If necessary, assign a lighting and stage crew. Also, recruit students to hand out programs and take care of other odd jobs.

Two Weeks Prior to Performance

1. All music should be memorized. The remaining rehearsals should be for "polish" and performance procedure review.

2. List the order of the program on a chalkboard. Expect children to know this order.

3. If possible, rehearse mounting the risers. Help children realize that the way they enter and exit the performance area will affect the quality of their performance. While students are on the risers there should be no primping or talking. Eyes should be on the director at all times.

4. Prepare the program format and submit it to a typist or school secretary.

5. Assign students to be responsible for any instruments or special props to be used.

One Week Prior to Performance

1. Double-check any travel arrangements.

2. Instruct chorus members about what to do if they become ill during the performance. At this age, it is not unusual for one or two students to become faint. Ask a parent to bring tissues, smelling salts, and a damp cloth. Be prepared!

3. If you wish, request your school media specialist, a parent, or an audio-visual crew to tape the concert.

4. Review with chorus members the time and place of the concert as well as what they are to wear.

5. Request that students give themselves "voice rest." For ten- and eleven-year-olds this means less yelling in gym and on the playground.

The Day of the Performance

1. Arrive early to see that the stage or performance area is in order, programs are ready to be distributed, and the warm-up area is prepared.

2. If you are traveling by school bus, encourage children to keep talking to a minimum. Trying to talk above the roar of school bus engines is a good way to insure voice strain.

3. Remind children that their behavior and noise level before a performance creates an important first impression. Also, leaving the performance area should be quiet and orderly.

4. Rehearsal on the day of a performance should be very light. If you feel you have to have a "crash" rehearsal the day of the performance, you shouldn't be performing!

5. Try to insure that as many details as possible have been taken care of. Despite the best-made plans, sometimes things just don't go as you expected....buses are late, lights don't work, programs don't arrive, the accompanist drops the music. Prepare children and yourself to expect the unexpected and to do your best no matter what!

Stage Deportment

No matter how well your children sing, their overall performance can be enhanced by poised stage deportment. Children who are attentive and confident during performance are not only more appealing to watch, but they sing better too. From the first rehearsal, the development of a sense of pride and attention to detail should build the foundation for this. As performance dates approach, specifics of good deportment should be taught and rehearsed.

Remember, most children have had very little experience performing. Therefore, take nothing for granted. Before any performance, review the following:

1. Performance begins the moment you leave the warm-up area. There should be no talking or "horseplay" in the halls or the performance area.

2. There should be no primping during performance. Combing hair and adjusting clothing should be done in the warm-up area.

3. Rehearse a quiet and orderly procedure for getting on and off the stage and/or risers. Appoint row leaders and be sure they know exactly where to go.

4. Review correct singing posture. Good posture is basic to good performance. It says with body language, "We care."

5. Children are often distracted by the audience, especially when it includes friends and family members. Therefore, stress the importance of everyone focusing attention on the director. Make a humorous poster reading "All Eyes on the Director" to be used in final rehearsals. Emphasize the importance of this by asking students who fail to watch during final rehearsals to be seated until they can give you their complete attention.

6. It is important to let your audience know you enjoy performing for them. This does not mean, however, teaching children to wear a forced grin as they sing. Instead help children perceive performance as the culmination of all their efforts, a time to enjoy the benefits of their hard work. As you direct, relax and enjoy every moment. Chances are children will not only follow your musical cues, but your attitude and appearance as well.

7. During applause and between numbers, let children know they should relax a bit. Of course, this does not mean a time to talk, but rather, a time to shift body weight, flex the knees, and take a few deep breaths. Children often become so intent during performance, they forget to relax unless reminded to do so.

8. Be sure children understand cues for singing readiness. For instance, before beginning the next number, raise your arms slightly, holding them in position until you have everyone's attention. Do not begin the first downbeat until all eyes are on you. Likewise, during interludes or codas, be sure children know they are to remain attentive.

9. Review with children what should be done if someone becomes ill or faint.

10. A performance is not ended until the last chorus member leaves the performance area. Even then, it may be necessary to remind some groups that this is not a time to "whoop and holler." A beautiful performance can end on a sour note if students forget their stage manners too soon.

Making Travel Arrangements

It is usually best to wait until at least December of the school year for any outside-of-school performances. It takes the months preceding this to help children develop their readiness for such an outing. In fact, most out-of-school performances are best scheduled in the spring.

All out-of-school performances should be cleared by your school administration. Submit a detailed field trip description to the appropriate administrator, informing him or her of when, where, what, and why you will be performing. Be sure to include how the trip will be financed and any other important information. Once you have confirmed the date and time, be sure they are placed on the school calendar and that any teachers whose classes may be disrupted are informed of the plans.

A notice should be prepared to go home to parents. Once again, clearly explain when, where, what, and why. Explain what form of transportation will be used and if children will need to bring a lunch or will need money for any reason. Before any child is allowed to participate in an out-of-school performance, he or she must have signed permission from a parent or guardian stating that he or she has read the notice and that the child has permission to attend. Be sure to keep an accurate account of who has returned these signed notices.

It is usually best to transport children via school bus for such performances. If you are using buses, be sure they are ordered at least a month in advance. Check again to be sure buses are reserved for your group the day before performance.

Students should be aware of appropriate bus behavior. In general, it is best to have students seated in some type of performance order on the bus. This will help to avoid confusion when you reach your destination. It is also important that on the way to performances students do not talk loudly or sing. Ask them to bring a book or quiet game they can play on the bus.

If you are leaving for trip at 10:30 A.M., be sure children know they are to be in the lobby and ready to board buses at 10:20 A.M. Always try to have several other adults with you on such trips. One adult for every ten to twelve students will be a tremendous help.

It is a nice gesture to invite a school administrator or the PTA president to attend out-of-school performances. It is good for them to see the chorus as an extension of the learning environment, reaching out into the community. Recognize these persons when they are in attendance.

In general, avoid long trips for your choir. Children tire easily and seldom perform at their best when they have traveled more than an hour or two. Occasionally, you may receive a very special invitation that involves many hours of travel or even necessitates overnight arrangements. Before accepting such an invitation, weigh carefully the benefits and drawbacks for your group. Will it be a good experience for you and your students? If the answer is "Yes," meet with your chorus parents and work out details. Request specific persons to be in charge of making arrangements. Things you will need to consider are:

a. How will you finance the trip?
b. What is the best means of transportation?
c. Who will chaperone?
d. Where will students stay? How will room assignments be handled?
e. How will meals be provided?
f. What will the rehearsal and performance schedule be?
g. What do you do if a child becomes ill?
h. What limitations will there be for luggage and personal items brought?
i. Will there be special expectations for student conduct and behavior?
j. What will children do when they are not rehearsing or performing?

PLANNING FOR SPECIAL PERFORMANCES

Traditionally, winter holiday and spring concerts are the primary performances given by elementary school choruses. When children have worked hard and prepared their music well, however, it is important for them to have other performance experiences. These performances should provide a learning experience for students and a service or benefit to others. Just as special rehearsals and "fun" activities must be carefully planned, special performances must be worked out in detail and should come at times that enhance the overall choral schedule. Some special performance opportunities you might consider include:

Singing in the Community

Is there a business complex, a senior citizens home, a hospital, or a local shopping mall where your group might perform? Plans for such performances should be made well in advance (two months) and some local publicity is desirable. Go to the performance area ahead of time to be sure there are adequate facilities and inform students of what to expect in advance.

It is best to plan this type of less formal performance following a major concert. Your first opportunity will most likely be following your winter holiday program. You should have an adequate and well prepared repertoire at this time and the addition of several familiar carols for a sing-a-long can round out an enjoyable program.

Singing for some community groups like a Garden Club or the local chapter of the American Association of University Women will require a more formal presentation. These performances are usually by invitation and should be accepted only if they come at times when you know your group will be adequately prepared.

Performing on Television

While it is very flattering to be invited to perform on television, the elementary choral teacher should be aware of some potential problems before accepting such an invitation. Taping a concert in a television studio takes a great deal of effort to insure a quality performance and good experience for youngsters.

First of all, most local television studios are not equipped to comfortably accommodate a large number of children. Therefore, go to the studio ahead of time to work out details with the person in charge of your production. Is there an adequate area for students to wait before their taping? Is there a piano? Is it in tune? Where will students perform? Are there adequate risers? Where are the rest-rooms? How long will the taping take?

When you have worked out details such as these, begin to familiarize students with what to expect. Explain the layout of the studio and with whom they will be working. Send notes home to parents requesting that children look their best and are dressed appropriately. Request that children have a light, nourishing meal before the taping. Ask chorus parents to have a snack ready for children when the taping is over.

Once inside the studio, children will be fascinated by the cameras, monitors, lights, and crew around them. Take a few minutes to introduce the director and to help children become acclimated to their new and unusual surroundings. Request several minutes to warm up in the studio. This will give both you and your students an opportunity to focus attention on singing before actual taping begins.

Perhaps the greatest problem with studio taping is the intense heat and glare of the lighting equipment. This may cause children who are already excited to become faint or ill. Be sure to have several chorus parents on hand and prepared to help out. Between takes, be sure children relax and cool down. If it is a particularly long taping, allow sufficient time for drinks and bathroom breaks.

Live performances taped by mini-cameras usually do not present the same problems as studio taping. However, children will tend to be distracted, and achieving a really fine performance may be difficult. Preparing children ahead of time for any type of filming is essential.

When the performance is aired on television, try to have it video-taped, if possible. Does your school system own the equipment to do this? If so, ask a media specialist to make the tape for you. If not, perhaps the family of a chorus member may have a video recorder that can be used.

Children enjoy seeing themselves perform. Therefore, plan a special time to get together to view the tape as a group. Finally, store the tape in your school media center so it can be enjoyed by others for years to come.

Participating in Choral Festivals

Two types of choral festivals are particularly valuable for the elementary school chorus: the all-elementary choral festival and the area festival. There should be no competition at either of these festivals. Their goal should be to give children an opportunity to hear and perform for each other. In junior high or high school when select choral groups are organized, competition may be useful, but at the elementary level the values of personal and group achievement, rather than competition, should be stressed.

Both of these types of festivals are usually planned with the considerable input of choral teachers. By helping to plan such activities you help to insure a worthwhile experience not only for your own chorus, but for all of the children involved.

Festivals are usually best scheduled in the spring when repertoire is more fully developed and group cohesion is at its peak. A late May or early June date is usually best and should be selected early in the school year. Because of the numbers of children involved, a school with a large performance area should be selected for the festival.

The all-elementary choral festival frequently includes all elementary school choruses in a small school district, or all elementary choruses in a certain area of a larger system. If more than seven or eight choruses are involved, the schedule of performance may need to be divided into two or more sections with four or five groups participating in each.

The number of pieces performed by each group should be limited to two or three. Student pianists or instrumentalists might perform between the choral performances. Information about how students will be seated, how they will approach and leave the performance area, and the overall festival format should be discussed with students well in advance.

While competition at such festivals is undesirable, adjudication by a person knowledgeable in elementary choral music may be helpful. Two sets of comments should be prepared: one for the choral teacher suggesting concrete ways the chorus might be improved and a second for students. Comments to students should be positive and encourage continued participation in choral singing.

The area choral festival is most frequently a joint concert presented by the elementary, middle or junior high, and high school choruses in one geographic area. This festival gives students and the community an opportunity to hear the choral music program as a continuum. The concert should begin with the elementary chorus and end with the most advanced high school group. Combined numbers might be included if performance space allows.

Seating and performance procedures should be worked out ahead of time and a combined rehearsal is a must. As with the all-elementary festival, the purpose of the area festival should be to share, not to compete.

Participating in Joint or Exchange Concerts

Exchange or joint concerts can occur between any two performing groups. This might involve another elementary school, junior high school, high school, college, community, or senior citizens chorus.

For joint performances it is usually best to have at least one rehearsal together. If combined numbers are to be performed, they should be adequately rehearsed at this time. Be sure logistics are carefully worked out and that the repertoire for the program is compatible. From the start, the directors involved should share responsibility for such items as selecting a concert theme, preparation of the written concert program, publicity, and teaching combined numbers.

Another idea that provides an excellent learning experience for children is a joint rehearsal with a fine college choir. Here, each group performs some of its repertoire for the other in an informal rehearsal setting. Elementary school boys are usually fascinated to hear adult basses and tenors and to realize someday their voices will sound the same. On the other hand, young adults are usually quite interested in hearing children perform. This is especially true when there are several music education majors in the choir who may soon be teaching children themselves.

Exchange concerts are especially enjoyable with another elementary chorus of similar ability. This might take place as part of an all-school assembly, or it might just involve chorus members. Another especially nice exchange concert can occur between the elementary school chorus and a senior citizens chorus. This is a wonderful way to help bridge the generation gap.

Performing at Music Conventions and Workshops

These types of performances present some interesting challenges, primarily to the choral teacher. It is never easy to perform before your peers, especially when you know they will be scrutinizing your work and your group's performance. A key to success in such situations is to value the quality of experience for your students above perfection in performance. When you work toward a positive experience for your students instead of impressing the audience, you are likely to accomplish both.

As with any special performance, be sure it comes at a time when your chorus will be performance ready. Consider travel arrangements that must be made and try to visit the performance area ahead of time, if possible.

In a workshop setting, try to share with others how you do what you do. Conducting an actual rehearsal is an excellent activity for accomplishing this.

Chapter 9
Other Responsibilities of the Choral Teacher

CONDUCTING THE ELEMENTARY SCHOOL CHORUS

Good conducting is just as important for the elementary school chorus as it is for a select adult ensemble. While choral technique, literature selected, and rehearsal procedures will differ for adult and children's choirs, clear expressive conducting is essential to both.

Fortunately, choral conducting is a skill that can be learned. However, like playing a musical instrument, it is best learned by observing and working with someone who is highly skilled at the task. While reading about conducting is helpful, there is no substitute for working with a skilled conductor, accompanied by consistent practice.

The conducting tips presented here are basic and intended to encourage you to further develop your conducting skills. If you are comfortable with the materials mentioned here, you are ready for more in-depth work in conducting. If you find this material challenging, however, you will probably benefit from taking a course in basic conducting.

What Is Good Conducting?

Good choral conducting is the ability of the director to render the most musically accurate and expressive performance possible by his or her performing group. This involves (1) accurate intonation, (2) precise rhythm, (3) clear diction, (4) appropriate tempo and dynamics, (5) good tone color, (6) expressive phrasing, (7) appropriate balance and blend, and (8) an overall sense of cohesion that brings all of these elements together in an expressive whole.

Learning Basic Conducting Patterns

For many inexperienced directors, choral conducting is merely a matter of beating out the correct standard conducting pattern. While it is important to become familiar and comfortable with these patterns, they are only one ingredient among many for successful choral conducting. These basic patterns include the following.

Basic Right-Hand Conducting Patterns

The One-Beat Pattern. This pattern is basically a strong single downbeat followed by a rebound. (See Figure 9–1.) It is used for music with $\frac{3}{4}$, $\frac{3}{8}$, and fast $\frac{2}{2}$ or $\frac{2}{4}$ meters.

1

Figure 9–1

The Two-Beat Pattern. The two-beat pattern (see Figure 9–2) involves a strong downward movement followed by a weaker upward movement. It is used for music in $\frac{2}{4}$, ₵, $\frac{2}{2}$, and $\frac{6}{8}$ meter.

1

Figure 9–2

The Three-Beat Pattern. The three-beat pattern is used for $\frac{3}{4}$, $\frac{3}{2}$, $\frac{9}{8}$, and slow $\frac{3}{8}$ meters. It consists of a strong downward motion followed by a weaker motion to the right and a final upbeat. (See Figure 9–3.)

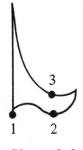

Figure 9–3

The Four-Beat Pattern. This pattern is the most common and is sometimes designated by C for "common time." Meters in $\frac{4}{4}$, $\frac{4}{8}$, $\frac{12}{8}$, and slow $\frac{2}{2}$ use this four-beat pattern. The components of the pattern are (1) a strong downward motion, (2) a weaker motion to the left, (3) crossing over the midpoint with a weaker motion to the right, and (4) the final upbeat. (See Figure 9–4.)

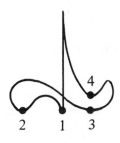

Figure 9–4

The Six-Beat Pattern. This pattern is used for music with a slow tempo in $\frac{6}{8}$ meter. Its components are (1) a strong downward motion, (2) a smaller motion left, (3) another short motion left, (4) a slightly accented and longer motion right, (5) a short motion right, and (6) a final upbeat. (See Figure 9–5.)

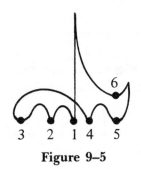

Figure 9–5

Some choral conductors argue that the consistent use of these patterns tends to make music mechanistic and that the real flow of the musical line should influence conducting gestures. In most cases, it is best to use these basic patterns while taking certain expressive liberties. For example, you may wish to suspend a basic pattern when you carry over or extend a phrase. This might be accomplished by using a smooth circular motion toward your group beginning at least one beat before the end of the first phrase. At an appropriate place in the next phrase, you would resume the conducting pattern.

It is also important that conducting patterns do not become "jerky" or abrupt. A fluid motion is most desirable and will help render a more expressive vocal line. For the best legato singing, smooth arm and hand movement by the conductor are essential.

Using Cues and Gestures

Along with using fluid conducting patterns, the choral teacher must be able to provide a variety of musical cues and gestures. Some of the most important are included here:

Conductor's Gesture	Desired Response
1. Singing posture assumed; arms extended at shoulder height with elbows slightly bent.	1. Singing posture assumed; attention focused on the conductor; ready to sing.
2. Small but definite upward preparatory beat accompanied by a deep breath.	2. Synchronized inhalation by all singers.
3. The initial downbeat.	3. The precise articulation of the first sound.
4. Left-hand index finger in the air.	4. Preparation for upcoming entry.

Conductor's Gesture	*Desired Response*
5. A quick downward motion of the hands ending with a precise twist.	5. Clean, exact cut-off.
6. Thumb and forefinger quickly moved together and released.	6. Precise cut-off, entrance, or articulation of consonants.
7. Use of a large conducting pattern.	7. Loud dynamics.
8. Use of a small conducting pattern.	8. Soft dynamics.
9. A pulling motion, away from the body with an open hand.	9. To extend a phrase or to vitalize a held note.
10. Looking toward a particular section.	10. Preparation for an upcoming cue.
11. A nod of the head.	11. May indicate cut-off or entrance.
12. Index finger briefly over lips.	12. Softer dynamic level.
13. Increasing size of the conducting pattern accompanied by cupped hands and a slight lift of the elbows.	13. Crescendo.
14. Decreasing size of the conducting pattern accompanied by the relaxation of elbows.	14. Decrescendo.

Many choral teachers are most comfortable maintaining the conducting pattern with their right arm and hand and giving most cues with the left. While this is standard procedure, effective conducting may include any number of variations as long as it helps to enhance and does not detract from the overall performance.

Other Factors for Good Choral Conducting

Basic conducting patterns accompanied by clear cues and gestures form the basis for good choral conducting. There are, however, several other factors that can help to further enhance choral conducting and the creation of a rewarding musical experience.

First of all, it is important that the choral teacher knows thoroughly each score he or she will teach. Decisions about tempo, dynamics, and phrasing should be worked out before the first rehearsal. Once these decisions are made, the choral teacher must decide what conducting techniques will most clearly convey his or her interpretation. This interpretation should take into consideration the style and historical period of the piece, the composer's intentions as indicated in the score, the ability of the performing group, and the director's own musical judgment.

Begin to memorize your music as soon as possible. While it is helpful and necessary to use a score in rehearsal, the sooner music is memorized, the sooner you will be able to focus all of your attention on your singers. Music should always be memorized before performance, unless you are doing an extended or very difficult work. If you have never conducted without a score, challenge yourself to conduct at least one piece from memory on your next concert. You may be amazed at the level of rapport you are able to achieve with your chorus and the improvement you will find in overall performance.

Conducting in rehearsal and in performance will usually differ to some degree. In rehearsal, conducting gestures may be more exaggerated, while in performance a minimum amount of movement is desired. Just as children can memorize lyrics and notes, they can also learn to anticipate and memorize specific entrances and cut-offs, changes in dynamics and tempi, and subtle shifts in tone color. When these details have been carefully taught in rehearsal, the smallest gesture in performance may be all that is needed to recall what has been previously learned.

Body language is another important ingredient in choral conducting. Children often imitate the posture and energy level of their director. Therefore, the choral teacher whose body movements are vital and energetic will most likely have singers who appear and sound the same way. On the other hand, the teacher who seems to lack energy will probably have a group whose singing is lifeless and dull. The choral teacher who stands tall, breathes deeply, and takes great pleasure in performance will usually find his or her students mirror these desirable behaviors.

Finally, eye contact between the choral conductor and the chorus is essential. Never begin a number until you have everyone's eyes on you.

This eye contact is a primary factor in creating the cohesion necessary for good choral singing. From this visual contact, the conductor and his or her students should feel a bonding that moves together throughout the performance of a given composition. Lewis Gordon takes this notion a step further when he states, "The choral director should develop the constant image that he is connected by several strings with each member of the ensemble. Whenever he moves his hands, arms, or chest, there should be a physical feeling of directly controlling the singer's response."[1]

THE ACCOMPANIST

Qualities of a Good Accompanist

Good choral accompanists should have the technical facility to play accompaniments accurately and expressively. They should be adept at watching you while they play and should be able to follow your tempo and anticipate your cues. They should be sensitive to the appropriate balance needed between the accompaniment and singing. They should be sure of their own musicianship and enjoy and value choral accompanying.

Along with good musicianship, the accompanist for a children's choir should be someone who enjoys children and is supportive of you as the choral teacher. He or she should come to rehearsals and concerts prepared and must be willing to function as a member of the choral "team."

Selecting a Good Accompanist

No matter how rural, urban, or deprived your community may be, there is most likely someone qualified to accompany your chorus. While he or she may not be able to attend every rehearsal, there is usually another staff member, a parent, a friend, a local church musician, or an older student from the community who will be willing and able to help you.

If you are new in a community, ask your school administrator, another music teacher, or a local clergyman about accompanists in the

---

[1]Lewis Gordon, *Choral Director's Complete Handbook.* West Nyack, NY: Parker Publishing Company, Inc., 1977, p. 33.

area. Do they know of any local piano teachers you might contact? Is there a local organists' guild or an organization of church musicians that might have interested members? Once you have several names, contact these persons and explain your needs clearly. Above all, never ask someone to accompany whom you've never heard perform.

When you find someone who is interested, arrange a time together to go over selections from your repertoire for the coming year. Be sure to include one or two of your more challenging selections. Send some of this music to the potential accompanist ahead of time so he or she will have a chance to go over it before you meet. All good accompanists are not necessarily outstanding sight readers.

During your time together, go over the accompanied scores, noting tempo, dynamics, and any special directions you may have in mind. Conduct as the accompanist plays. Is he or she sensitive to your tempo and gestures? Are notes accurate? Is his or her playing expressive?

In essence, this person will be auditioning for you—auditioning for a nonpaying job. So, be careful to be positive in your manner. If his or her playing is not adequate, thank the person graciously for his or her time and explain you still have several persons to meet with before you make a decision. When you do find a person whose performance is to your liking, be sure he or she is able to attend all scheduled concerts and at least several rehearsals prior to these. Finding the best accompanist in the world is of little value if he or she cannot accompany your chorus in concert.

The Choral Teacher as Accompanist

Some elementary choral teachers prefer to accompany their choruses themselves. Perhaps this is because they are unsure of their conducting skills, or perhaps it is because they are truly unable to find a qualified accompanist. For whatever reasons, be assured that this practice detracts from the choral teacher's ability to direct and train young voices. Since hands, facial expressions, and body language are so important in effective vocal teaching and directing, the choral teacher should be at the piano as little as possible, especially in concerts and in final rehearsals. No matter how qualified the teacher may be as a pianist and accompanist, it rarely compensates for what is lost when his or her attention is divided between the chorus and the keyboard.

The primary focus of the choral teacher must be on the singers and the choral sound. The teacher who works from the keyboard is unable to move freely among the singers. He or she is less likely to hear subtle differences of tone and balance, and is unable to give expressive cues that often make the difference between mediocre and outstanding choral singing.

Of course, there are exceptions to this notion. Some very talented teachers are able to achieve outstanding vocal performance even when they accompany. These are usually very talented directors who teach so thoroughly in rehearsal that when they are at the keyboard during performance, little seems to be lost. This is extremely rare, however, especially with elementary school choruses.

Rehearsing Without an Accompanist

Children should not always be accompanied when they sing. As a matter of fact, it is desirable that they do a good bit of singing unaccompanied. This helps to build vocal independence and confidence. It helps to focus more attention on the specifics of singing.

From time to time, however, especially when learning a new piece, it is helpful to have parts played as children sing. If your accompanist is unable to attend every rehearsal, consider asking several chorus members who study piano to learn the alto or soprano part of particular pieces and to assist you in rehearsal. These rehearsal accompanists can be a great help.

Of course, it is important that all chorus members hear and are familiar with accompaniments well before performance. This can present a problem for teachers with limited keyboard skills or whose accompanists can attend only a few rehearsals prior to performance. In this type of situation, you might consider using rehearsal tapes. While far from ideal, these pre-taped accompaniments can provide students with the aural experience of hearing accompaniments and can free the choral teacher to direct during rehearsal.

If you use this approach, be sure accompaniments are taped exactly as you want them to sound in concert. This will require your careful knowledge and interpretation of the music before you get together with your accompanist to make the tape. When recording, be sure to use a high quality tape and a recorder that will render a clear and pleasing tone with adequate volume.

To use the tape effectively in rehearsal, write the name of each selection on an index card in the order the selections are recorded. Next to each title, write the calibration number and affix the index card to the tape player. When you wish to rehearse a particular song with accompaniment, run the tape to the desired number and begin.

Your hands will be free to conduct, your eyes will be able to focus on your students, and your ears will be able to listen attentively to the singing.

Student Accompanists

Student accompanists are often very helpful in rehearsals and delightful additions to the concert program. If you have several students who study piano, enlist them to assist you with warm-ups and learning parts as suggested earlier in this chapter. For more capable students, select a piece you know they will be able to play comfortably and ask them to learn the accompaniment. If possible, ask their piano teacher to help them study the piece. These kinds of experiences are great motivators for young pianists. They will do their best and may surprise you with their desire and ability to play such assignments.

If you have time, you may wish to have an "accompanist" class. This might include students who study piano or any other students who are interested in learning bell, rhythm, autoharp, guitar, or Orff accompaniments. The organization of this class should be flexible, varying instruction and students based on the type of accompaniments being learned.

Whatever accompanying instruments you decide to use, there is only one consideration that must always be met in performance—the accompaniments must enhance singing and never distract from it. The persons playing the accompaniment, be they students or adults, must render the accompaniment musically and in a manner that enhances the overall performance.

ORGANIZING OTHER SINGING EXPERIENCES FOR CHILDREN

Teaching "Chorus" in the Primary Grades

In the primary grades, kindergarten through grade three, careful consideration should be given regarding the need for a structured chorus experience for children. In most cases, children at this level are not ready for the type of choral program suggested here for older students. Many children still need much experience with vocal experimentation and some have not discovered the difference between their speaking and singing voices. Emphasis here should be on less structured singing games and activities. Children should be encouraged to move and experiment with their voices. This is not to say primary age choirs are never desirable, however. There are situations when careful planning based on the needs of a particular group of children can result in a positive group singing experience.

The two basic goals of a primary age chorus are: (1) to encourage a love of singing and (2) to help children develop their fullest vocal potential at their own stage of development. The nature of the first goal suggests that activities and materials be "fun." The second implies a need for as much small-group and individual attention as possible.

From the start, the idea of a group of fifty or sixty primary age children meeting for a weekly structured rehearsal seems inappropriate. While this is quite acceptable for older children, younger children generally do not respond positively to or need this type of setting. A more suitable approach might be to divide primary age children into small groups of ten to fifteen, meeting on a rotating basis for "Training Choir."

During a twenty- to thirty-minute period, children should participate in a variety of activities that will give them as much opportunity to sing as possible. Activities should include singing games with an emphasis on movement and individual singing response. Echo games and ear training should be basic components of the program. With this type of approach in mind, the choral teacher would be wise to make use of basic Kodály, Orff, or Tometic materials. These are fine resources for developing both listening and singing skills for young children.

Throughout the year, three or four songs might be prepared that are suitable for performance. By allowing plenty of time to learn music in the small-group setting, actual performance rehearsals can be kept to a minimum. Singing for a parent tea or visitation in the spring is usually a fine culminating experience.

With emphasis on informal small-group instruction in the primary grades, the choral teacher is more able to identify and assist children who need special help for optimum vocal development. With this additional help, by the time these children reach the upper elementary grades, they are much more likely to be successful singers.

In the most profound sense, the informal but carefully planned small-group singing experience in the primary grades can be the forerunner of a continuum of choral music education. Just as children must develop readiness for reading or math, so too the type of singing experience discussed here can ready children for an introduction to choral singing in the upper elementary grades. Ideally, individual and choral singing skills are further developed throughout junior and senior high school, the final result being adults who love to sing and who have developed their fullest singing potential.

Teaching Children's Church Choirs

The children's church choir is an excellent place to begin working with young singers. Depending on the size of the church and the number of children involved in the choir program, there may be many opportunities for providing singing experiences suitable for children at all levels. In larger churches this might include a cherub choir (4–5 year-olds), a primary choir (1st–3rd grades), a junior choir (4th–6th grades), a youth choir (junior and senior high school), and an adult choir. Most churches, regardless of their size, have an adult choir and this group can be strengthened considerably by the development of a choir program that will eventually feed members into it.

The goals of the children's church choir should be very similar to those mentioned for the elementary school chorus. However, they must also reflect the function of the choir as part of a religious community. Additional goals might include:

1. to help children learn and value sacred music,
2. to foster an understanding of worship,
3. to contribute something meaningful to the worship life of the church, and
4. to train future leaders of worship and music in the church.

The primary ingredient for a successful children's church choir is the same as for the elementary school chorus—a knowledgeable and enthusiastic director. Along with this, the support of the church staff and adequate financial resources are also essential. Parent involvement seems to be another helpful ingredient as are an appropriate rehearsal schedule and facility.

One of the biggest problems for church choirs seems to be finding a suitable rehearsal time and transportation for children. In some churches these problems are solved by having rehearsals on Sunday mornings as part of the overall church education program. In other instances rehearsals are held after school with a carpool of parents or a church van providing transportation.

Keeping children motivated to participate is another common problem among children's church choirs. Lively, well planned rehearsals, interesting and appropriately challenging music, opportunities to sing in worship and the community, and occasional extra musical activities can all help to maintain student interest. Attendance awards and recognition pins are also good motivators, as is attendance at summer choir camps or workshops.

While all of the information in this book dealing with the development of the child voice and choral technique is applicable to the children's church choir, it is beyond the scope of this book to deal with specific organizational matters. Therefore, anyone working with a children's church choir would be well served to learn about Choristers Guild. This is a nonprofit organization that strives to maintain the highest standards possible for children's and youth choirs in the church. It is a national organization with local chapters in over fifty areas of the United States and Canada. The organization sponsors excellent choral workshops and festivals. It publishes fine music and a newsletter that is filled with information and suggestions for working with the children's church choir. More information can be obtained by writing to Choristers Guild, whose address is found in Chapter 9.

Working with the Children's Community Chorus

As with the children's church choir, much of the information presented in this book can be used successfully with the children's community chorus. Depending on the age level involved, many of the teaching suggestions will be appropriate. Ideas for concert planning and the selection of music are also applicable. There are, however, some problems unique to the organization of a children's community chorus and they are discussed below.

Building Support and Financial Backing. When there has been no history of a children's community chorus, the interested choral teacher will need to develop a base of support before a program can be effectively developed. In some communities this support may come through a park district or community school recreation program. In some areas, successful community choirs have been the outgrowth of local church music programs. Music schools, colleges, and universities are sometimes the primary support for a community chorus, as are local musical organizations. Fine adult choirs will often lend support to children's choirs.

Before you approach one of these groups or institutions, work out the goals and objectives you foresee for the chorus. Be prepared to answer questions like, "What purpose will it serve?" "Who will be needed for staff?" "How many children will realistically be involved?" "What kind of budget will you need?" "How often will you rehearse?" "How often will you perform?" "What type of music will be performed?" Obtaining adequate support and financial backing will depend greatly on your ability to answer these kinds of questions.

Once you have established the support you need, organize a committee or "Board of Directors" to initiate policy and plans for the future. Put goals and objectives on paper and assign tasks that will help achieve those goals.

Determining Membership Criteria. Will the community chorus be a select group of top-notch singers or will it be a "singing for fun group" composed of anyone who wants to sing? Will it include elementary and junior high students? Will boys whose voices are changing or have changed be included? Will membership be limited to a set number of participants? Will there be a membership fee?

There are no specific answers to these questions. They will vary depending upon your community and the goals you and your committee have established. Whatever they may be, put the membership criteria you have determined on paper and use it to help plan appropriate recruitment activities.

Recruiting Members. If your goal is to develop an outstanding performing group, it may be a good idea to visit local school and church choir directors to learn about outstanding students. You will need the support of these directors if you are to interest the best students possible. In this type of situation, students might be "nominated" by their teachers to audition for the chorus. It would be considered an honor to be nominated and chosen to participate.

On the other hand, if your goal is to provide an opportunity for as many students as possible to sing, posters and announcements in the local newspaper may be adequate. Notices might be distributed through local schools or a recreation program if it is sponsoring the chorus.

Building Group Morale. Nothing builds group morale as effectively as pride in performance. As the chorus develops a fine reputation in the community and elsewhere, "belonging" takes on a special significance for children who are proud to be a part of the group.

Along with pride in performance, it is important to nurture friendships among the members. Many children may come from different schools and will need informal opportunities to get to know one another. Therefore, allow times when children can talk and play together. Ask parents to provide refreshments from time to time, allowing children an opportunity to socialize. Organize a few special social events through the year like picnics or holiday parties to complement the rehearsal and performance schedule.

DEVELOPING PROFESSIONAL RESOURCES

Recommended Reading

While little has been written about teaching choral music in the elementary school, there are several books and articles most elementary choral teachers will find helpful. They are listed here by general topic.

Development of the Child Voice and Singing

Music: A Way of Life for the Young Child
  by Kathleen Bayless and Marjorie Ramsey
  The C.V. Mosby Co., St. Louis, MO, 1978
Music Learning
  by Marion Flagg
  C. C. Birchard and Co., Boston, MA, 1949
Music in the Elementary School (4th Edition)
  by Vernice Nye and Robert Nye
  Prentice-Hall, Inc., Englewood Cliffs, NJ, 1977
Your Children Need Music
  by Marvin Greenberg
  Prentice-Hall, Englewood Cliffs, NJ, 1979

Working with Underdeveloped Singers

"Help for Inaccurate Singers"
  by Samuel L. Forcucci
  Music Educators Journal, October 1975, pp. 57–61
Music Learning
  (See above)
The Psychology of Music Teaching (Chapter VI)
  by Edwin Gordon
  Prentice-Hall, Englewood Cliffs, NJ, 1971
"The Uncertain Singer"
  by Austin Lovelace
  Choristers Guild Letters, February 1977, pp. 111–112

Working with Children's Choirs

Music in Church Education with Children
  by Helen Kemp
  Choristers Guild, Dallas, TX, 1975

The Children's Choir—Vol. I
   by Ruth Jacobs
   Fortress Press, Philadelphia, PA, 1957
The Children's Choir—Vol. II
   by Nancy Poore Tufts
   Fortress Press, Philadelphia, PA, 1965
The Successful Children's Choir
   by Ruth K. Jacobs
   H. T. Fitzsimons, Chicago, IL, 1948
Vocal Techniques for Children and Youth
   by Ingram and Rice
   Abingdon Press, Nashville, TN, 1962

Vocal Technique

Choral Music Education (Chapters IV and V)
   by Paul F. Roe
   Prentice-Hall, Englewood Cliffs, NJ, 1970
Complete Handbook of Voice Training
   by Richard Alderson
   Parker Publishing Company, West Nyack, NY, 1979
Expressive Singing, Third Edition—Vol. I
   by Van A. Christy
   Wm. C. Brown Company, Dubuque, IA, 1974

Choral Conducting

Choral Directing
   by Wilhelm Ehmann
   Augsburg, Minneapolis, MN, 1968
Choral Director's Complete Handbook, (Chapter I)
   Lewis Gordon
   Parker Publishing Company, Inc., West Nyack, NY, 1977
Choral Music Education (Chapter VIII)
   (see above)

Attending Choral Workshops

Another excellent way to learn more about teaching children's choirs is to attend choral workshops. Several colleges that have offered summer programs dealing with the child voice and children's choirs are listed here. If you are interested in attending an elementary choral workshop, write to these schools to see if they presently have such an offering.

   Hartt School of Music
     University of Hartford
     West Hartford, CT 06117

Holy Names College
   3500 Mountain Boulevard
   Oakland, CA 94619

Ithaca College
   School of Music
   Ithaca, NY 14850

Westminster Choir College
   Princeton, NJ 08540

Local chapters of Choristers Guild and Kodály Educators also offer choral workshops from time to time. These are usually one- or two-day sessions available to members and non-members alike.

Professional Organizations

Each of the organizations listed here provides information and education for choral teachers. Each publishes a helpful journal or newsletter that deals with many aspects of music education. For more information about each, write to the addresses below:

American Choral Directors Association
   P.O. Box 6310
   Lawton, OK 73506

American Orff-Schulwerk Association
   Department of Music
   Cleveland State University
   Cleveland, OH 44115

Choristers Guild
   2834 W. Kingsley Road
   Garland, TX 75041

Music Educators National Conference
   1902 Association Drive
   Reston, VA 22091

National Association of Teachers of Singing
   c/o New York University
   35 West Fourth Street
   Room 778
   New York, NY 10003

Organization of American Kodály Educators
   Robert Perinchief
   OAKE Executive Secretary
   University of Wisconsin–Whitewater
   Whitewater, WI 53190

A Directory of Publishers

To stay abreast of the latest choral publications, write to publishers for their catalogues and reference copies of their music. Some companies provide recordings as well as copies of their publications for a membership fee.

Augsburg Publishing House
426 South Fifth Street
Minneapolis, MN 55415
Belwin-Mills Publishing Corporation
25 Deshon Drive
Melville, NY 11746
Big Three Music Corporation
(See Columbia Pictures Publications)
Joseph Boonin, Inc.
(See European American Music Corp.)
Boosey and Hawkes, Inc.
200 Smith Street
Farmingdale, NY 11735
Bourne, Inc.
1212 Avenue of the Americas
New York, NY 10036
Broadman Music Press
127 Ninth Avenue, North
Nashville, TN 37303
Alexander Broude, Inc.
225 West 57th Street
New York, NY 10019
Canyon Press
P.O. Box 12135
Cincinnati, OH 45201
Chappell and Company
(See Hal Leonard)
Choristers Guild
(See Lorenz Industries)
Columbia Pictures Publications
P.O. Box 4340
16333 N.W. 54th Avenue
Hialeah, FL 33014
Concordia Publishing House
3558 South Jefferson Avenue
St. Louis, MO 63118
Coronet Press
(See Alexander Broude)
European American Music Corp.
11 West End Road
Totowa, NJ 07512

Carl Fischer, Inc.
    56–62 Cooper Square
    New York, NY 10003
J. Fischer and Brother
    (See Belwin-Mills)
Harold Flammer, Inc.
    (See Shawnee Press)
Mark Foster Music Company
    P.O. Box 4012
    Champaign, IL 61820
Hinshaw Music, Inc.
    P.O. Box 470
    Chapel Hill, NC 27514
Hope Publishing Company
    380 South Main Place
    Carol Stream, IL 60187
Jenson Publications, Inc.
    2880 S. 171 Street
    New Berlin, WI 53151
Kendor Music, Inc.
    P.O. Box 278
    Main and Grove Streets
    Delevan, NY 14042
Neil A. Kjos Publishing Corp.
    4382 Jutland Drive
    San Diego, CA 92117
Lorenz Industries
    501 East Third Street
    Dayton, OH 45401
Hal Leonard Music
    8112 West Bluemound Road
    Milwaukee, WI 53213
Magnamusic-Baton, Inc.
    10370 Page Industrial Blvd.
    St. Louis, MO 63132
Edward B. Marks Music Corp.
    (See Belwin-Mills)
Mercury Music Corp.
    (See Theodore Presser Co.)
Oxford University Press
    16-00 Pollitt Drive
    Fair Lawn, NJ 07410
Plymouth Music Company, Inc.
    170 N.E. 33rd Street
    Ft. Lauderdale, FL 33334
Theodore Presser Co.
    Presser Place
    Bryn Mawr, PA 19010

Pro Art Publications, Inc.
    (See Belwin-Mills)
Robbins Music
    (See Columbia Pictures Publications)
Sacred Music Press
    501 East Third Street
    P.O. Box 802
    Dayton, OH 45401
E. C. Schirmer Music Company
    112 South Street
    Boston, MA 02111
G. Schirmer Inc.
    866 Third Avenue
    New York, NY 10022
Schmitt, Hall, and McCreary Company
    (See Belwin-Mills)
Schott and Company
    (See European American Music Corp.)
Shawnee Press
    Delaware Water Gap, PA 18327
Somerset Press
    (See Hope Publishing Company)
Southern Music Company
    P.O. Box 329
    1100 Broadway
    San Antonio, TX 78292
Studio P/R
    (See Columbia Pictures Publications)
Walton Music Corporation
    (See Lorenz Industries)

INDEX

A

A capella singing, 112, 115-117
Accompanists, 191-194
Administrators, gaining support of, 15-16
Adolescence, and voice changes, 33
Advanced students, 18
Articulation, 75, 76
    sibilants, 80
    See also Diction
Assistants, student, 56, 155
    accompanists, 194
Auditory memory, 30, 31, 32
Awards assembly, 159-160

B

Balance, achieving, 104-105
    activities, 106-108
Ball, Larry K., 93
Beer, Alice, 146
Blend, requirements, 105-106
    activities, 107
Breathing, proper, 31, 32, 70-74
    controlled, teaching, 72-74
    deep, teaching, 70-71
    normal vs. singing, 70
    poor habits, effect of on tone, 101-102
    shallow breathing, 71
    staggered breathing, 73, 109

C

Caroling party, 159
Chanting, 28, 29
Chest voice, 30, 31, 55, 62-64
    head voice, comparison to, 63

Child-centered choral music, 4, 8, 16-17
Children's choirs, characteristics, 52
Choral singing:
    goals, 4
    reasons for teaching, 3-4
    size of group, 18
    support groups, 15-17
    See also Performances; Rehearsals; Teacher,
        choral
Choristers Guild, 19
Church choirs, children's, 196-197
Classroom management, 152-156
    chorus helpers, 155
    discipline, 155-156
    guidelines for behavior, 153
    lesson planning, 152-153
    rehearsal routines, 154
    seat assignments, 153
    tempo, 155
    vocal scores, selecting, 152
Colleagues, gaining support, 16
Community chorus, children's, 197-199
Community groups, performances for, 180
Concerts, *see* Performances
Conducting, 185-191
    cues and gestures, 188-189
    patterns, 186-188
Consonants, 75, 76, 77, 80-81
    aspirate "h", 81
    final, 94-95
    percussive, 81
    "r", 81-82, 95-96
    "s", 96-97
    scooping, 93-94
    sustaining, 80
    "the", 82
    vowels vs., teaching difference, 84-85
    See also Diction

D

Developmental characteristics of children, grades 1-8, 5-6
See also Voice development
Diction, 30, 31, 32, 52, 55, 75-99
  common problems, 81-82
  consonants, 76-77, 80-81, 81-82
  diphthongs, 77, 79-80, 92-93
  recommended sources, 82-83
  scooping, 80, 83, 93-94
  sloppy, effect of on tone, 102
  speech vs. singing, 76
  teaching, 83-99
  vowels, 76, 77-80, 83-93
Diphthongs, 77, 79-80, 92-93, 143
  See also Diction; Vowels
Discipline, 155-156

E

Echoing activities, 28, 29, 39, 43, 44, 45, 46-47, 61, 109
  teaching echo-type songs, 126-127
Eligibility for chorus, determining, 17-18
End-of-the-year picture and party, 159
Enunciation, 75, 76
  See also Diction
Exchange or joint concerts, 183
Expressive singing, 112-115
  dynamic contrasts, 113-114
  meaning of songs, helping children to understand, 112
  metronome, use of, 115
  tempo changes, 114

F

Festivals, choral, 181-183
Field trips, 158-159
  permission slips, 175
  travel arrangements for, 178-179
Finances, 9
  budget proposals, 21-22, 24
  sources of support, 22-23
Flagg, Marian, and four-step process for development of vocal accuracy, 44
Flatting, 108, 109, 111
"Flex" periods in teaching schedule, 13

G

Glissandos, 39, 47
"Glottal attack," 91
Goals:
  instructional, 7, 8
  personal, 7-8
Gordon, Edwin, 38
Greenberg, Marvin, 25

H

Harmony, development, 29, 30, 31, 107, 118, 138
  music selection, 163-164
  vertical, 130-137
Head voice, 30, 31, 32, 33, 40, 52, 53, 62-66
  activities for developing, 64-66
  chest vs. head voice, differences, 63
Hearing, "inner" and "outer," 39, 42, 43, 109
Holidays, 14, 144, 157, 162
  concert themes, 69-70
  performances, special, 179
  program, sample, 172
Instructional goals, 7, 8
Intonation, 108-112
  suggestions for developing, 108-112

K

Kemp, Helen, 46
Kindergarten singers, nurturing vocal development, 28-29
Kodàly approach, 45, 116, 118, 150
  hand signs, 61, 136

L

Lesson plans, 8, 152-153
  writing, 144, 146
Libraries, choral, 23
Listening skills:
  activities for, 42-43, 60-62
  "Listening Song, The," 60
  students, developing, 59-62
  teacher, 58-59

M

Melodies, helping children identify and sing, 28, 29, 44-45, 107, 118-119, 124
 countermelodies, 127-129
 melody bells, 44
 music selection, 163
Memorization, 150-151
Modeling, choral teacher, 54-56, 57
Music selection, 152, 161-168
 accompaniment, 164-165
 harmony, 163-164
 level of difficulty, 164
 lyrics, 161-162
 melody, 163
 range, 162-163
 suggestions, 166-168
 suitability, 165
 tessitura, 162

N

Notation, musical, 115, 149-150
Notebook, establishment of for chorus, 8-9

O

Organization of American Kodàly Educators, 45
Ostinatos, 117, 118-119, 121, 122, 126
"Out-of-tune" singers, 17

P

Parents:
 chaperones, 175, 179
 fathers, 21
 support of, 16
 trips, 179
 as volunteers, 12, 16, 56, 138, 181
Part singing, 109, 118-139
 countermelodies, 127-129
 echo-type songs, 126-127
 ostinatos, 118-119, 122
 partner songs, 129-130
 rounds, 121-122, 124
 song suggestions, 125-126
 vertical harmony, 130-137
Performances, 10, 105, 143
 planning step-by-step, 174-176

Performances (*cont'd*)
 preparation, 161-184
 program building, 170-174
 schedules, sample, 11, 157
 scheduling, 14
 special, planning for, 179-184
 stage deportment, 176-178
 themes, 169-170
 travel arrangements, 175, 176, 178-179, 184
 See also Music selection
Permission slips, 175, 178
Physical problems, effect of on singing, 40, 41
Pitch accuracy, development, 28, 29, 30, 37, 41
 underdeveloped singers, 37
Pitch-making, activities, 43-44, 45
Posture, singing, 30, 32, 34, 66-70, 177
 poor posture, effect of on tone, 100
 suggestions for teaching, 67-70
Preschool voice development, 25-27
Primary grades, teaching chorus, 194-196
Principal:
 preparation for meeting with, 10
 role of, 15
Professionalism, and gaining support of others, 15
Professional organizations, 201
Programs, printed, 174, 175
Pronunciation, 75
 See also Diction
Publishers, choral publications, 202-204

R

Recordings of children's choirs, 52-53, 56
Recruitment of chorus members, 19-21
 boys, 20-21
 "pre-chorus" rehearsal, 20
 voice assessments, 19-20
Rehearsals, 10, 12, 56-57, 58-59, 113, 143-160
 à capella, 116, 117
 area for, 152
 "boys only", 66
 breathing, 72-73
 classroom management, 152-156
 conducting, 190
 diction, 83
 events calendar, sample, 157
 first, 156
 objectives, 143-146
 "pre-chorus," 20

Rehearsals (*cont'd*)
    tapes, 138, 193
    techniques, 147-151
    theme, 157-158
    without accompaniment, 58, 147, 193-194
Remedial instruction, 41-47
Repertoire, 14, 28, 30, 31, 32
    See also Music selection
Resources, professional, 199-200
Rounds, 121-122, 124
    song suggestions, 125-126

S

Scheduling, 9-14
    performances, 14
    rehearsals, 10, 12-13
    sample schedule, 11
    sectionals and special groups, 13
    voice assessments, 13-14
Scooping, 80, 83, 93-94
Sharping, 108, 109
Sibilants, 80, 96-97
Sight reading, 147, 149-150, 151
Sliding, 80, 93
Solfége, 61, 136
Solo singing, 31, 32
Songs, new, introducing, 147-149
"Sound ideal," developing, 51-52
    communicating, 54, 56-58
Speaking vs. singing voice, 27, 28, 29
    activities for finding singing voice, 45-46
    speechlike singer, 39-40, 41
Stage deportment, 176-178

T

Teacher, choral:
    as accompanist, 192-193
    assessing choir's potential, 53-54
    as conductor, 185-191
    listening skills, 58-59
    as model, 54-56
    role of, 51
    skills needed, 7
    sound ideal, 51-52, 54, 56-58
    voice instruction, 55
Television performances, 180-181
Tessitura, 108-109, 162

Tometics, 150
Tonal memory, 27, 30
    methods for developing, 44-45
Tonal vocabulary, 20, 31, 32, 37, 39, 41
Tone quality, developing, 100-104
    activities, 102-104
    distortion, causes:
        breathing habits, poor, 101
        diction, sloppy, 102
        focus, lack of, 101-102
        poor posture, 100-101
        tension, 100
Trust, fostering attitude of, 58

U

Underdeveloped singers, 17-18, 37
    dependent, 38-39
    limited-range, 40
    remedial classes, 31, 32
    speechlike, 39-40
    untuned, 40-41
    working with, 41-47
Unison singing, 30, 31, 32, 41, 43

V

Vocal range:
    activities for expanding, 46-47
    determination, 35
    development, 26, 27, 28-29, 30, 32, 40, 43
    music selection, 162-163
    tension, effect of, 40
Vocal skills, evaluation, 34-37
    group, 37
    vocal interview form, 36
Voice assessments, 13-14, 19-20
Voice changes, 33-34, 66
Voice development, 25-47
Voice instruction, for teachers, 55
Voice quality, 30
Vowels, 75, 76, 77-80, 102, 104, 109
    AH, 78
    vs. consonants, teaching difference, 84-85
    dipthongs, 77, 79-80, 92-93
    EE, 77-78
    EH, 78
    initial, 91-92
    modifying, 89-90
    OH, 78

Vowels (*cont'd*)
    OO, 78-79
    teaching, 85-89
        tall, 86, 102
    uniform, 90-91
    See also Diction

W

Workshops:
    attending, 200-201
    performances, 183-184